STUDENT STUDY GUIDE

Ellen G. Cohn, Ph.D.

Florida International University

Criminology Today

An Integrative Introduction

FIFTH EDITION

Frank Schmalleger, Ph.D.

Professor Emeritus
The University of North Carolina at Pembroke

Merrill
is an imprint of

PEARSON

Upper Saddle River, New Jersey
Columbus, Ohio

Editor in Chief: Vernon R. Anthony
Senior Editor: Tim Peyton
Development Editor: Elisa Rogers
Editorial Assistant: Alicia Kelly
Project Manager: Stephen C. Robb
Production Coordination: Emily Bush, S4Carlisle Publishing Services
Art Director: Mary Siener
Cover Design: Robert Aleman
Cover Image: Fotoresearch and Getty Images
Photographer: (Getty) Shooting Star
Operations Supervisor: Patricia A. Tonneman
Director of Marketing: David Gesell
Marketing Manager: Adam Kloza
Marketing Coordinator: Alicia Dysert

This book was set in Minion by S4Carlisle Publishing Services. It was printed and bound by Bind-Rite
Graphics, Inc. The cover was printed by Phoenix Color Corp.

Pearson Education Ltd.
Pearson Education Singapore Pte. Ltd.
Pearson Education Canada, Ltd.
Pearson Education—Japan

Pearson Education Australia Pty. Limited
Pearson Education North Asia Ltd.
Pearson Educación de Mexico, S.A. de C.V.
Pearson Education Malaysia Pte. Ltd.

Merrill
is an imprint of

10 9 8 7 6 5 4 3
ISBN-13: 978-0-13-513501-3
ISBN   0-13-513501-X

Contents

Part VI   Crime in the Modern World

Introduction—To the Student

Welcome to the field of criminology! This study guide has been designed to supplement your textbook, *Criminology Today: An Integrative Introduction*, by Frank Schmalleger. It is **not** intended to be a substitute for reading and studying the textbook! Please read each chapter in the textbook in addition to using the study guide. To get the most out of both your textbook and study guide, you may want to follow these steps when studying each chapter:

1. First, review the learning outcomes, which are found in both the textbook and the study guide. They provide you with goals, so keep them in mind while you study the chapter.
2. Next, read through the chapter outline and chapter summary provided in the study guide to obtain an overview of the chapter's contents. Remember: Reading the chapter summary in the study guide is not the same as reading the chapter in the textbook!
3. Now it is time to read the chapter in your textbook. While reading, try to keep in mind the various issues that are raised in the learning outcomes.
4. Review the key terms found in your study guide. Use them to solve the word search and crossword puzzles in the study guide.
5. Go back to the learning outcomes at the beginning of the chapter. Now that you have read the chapter in the textbook, see if you can meet these objectives. If not, review the relevant sections in the chapter.
6. Look at the questions for review and questions for reflection. Try to answer these questions.
7. Try to complete the student study guide questions without referring to the text for help or looking at the answers (which are provided in an appendix at the back of the study guide). This self-test includes true/false, fill-in-the-blank, and multiple-choice questions and will help you determine how well you have learned the material in this chapter. If you do not do well on the self-test, you may want to review the chapter and study guide materials again.

The study guide also contains several student exercises in each chapter. Your professor may assign these as homework or extra credit assignments. It also includes a list of related Web sites. You may wish to explore these sites to obtain more information on the topics covered in the chapter.

On a personal note, I hope that you will find this study guide to be both helpful and enjoyable. If you have any suggestions or ideas as to how this manual may be improved, please feel free to e-mail me with your comments. Enjoy your study of criminology!

Ellen G. Cohn, Ph.D.
Florida International University
cohne@fiu.edu

1 What Is Criminology?

Learning Outcomes

After reading this chapter, students should be able to:

- List the four definitional perspectives found in contemporary criminology, and relate the definition of *crime* used in this textbook
- Recognize the difference between acts that are criminal and those that are deviant, and explain how some forms of behavior can be both
- Understand the legalistic approach to the study of crime and explain how it can be used to decide what human activity is criminal
- Describe what criminologists do
- Offer an informed definition of *criminology*
- Explain how contemporary criminology sometimes influences social policy, especially in the area of crime control
- Describe the theme of this text, and be able to distinguish between the social problems and social responsibility perspectives on crime causation
- Describe the social context within which crime occurs, and identify the people and groups that are most affected by it
- Explain the interdisciplinary nature of criminology, while identifying reasons for the primacy of sociological approaches in the field today

Chapter Outline

Chapter Summary

Chapter 1 provides an introduction to the textbook and to the field of criminology. It begins by discussing various perspectives for defining crime, including the legalistic, political, sociological, and psychological viewpoints. The definition used in the text is from the legal perspective, which sees crime as "human conduct in violation of the criminal laws of a state, the federal government, or a local jurisdiction that has the power to make such laws." This approach does have some limitations, however, some of which may be addressed by the other perspectives on crime.

While many crimes are forms of deviant behavior, behavior that violates social norms, not all crimes are deviant and not all deviant behavior is criminal. There is also a significant difference between what *is* criminal and what *should be* criminal. The consensus perspective holds that a law should be developed to criminalize a certain behavior when the members of a society generally agree that such a law is necessary. However, in a multicultural society, consensus may be difficult to achieve. The diversity of society is recognized in the pluralistic perspective, which suggests that behaviors are typically criminalized through a political process after debate over the appropriate course of action.

This chapter also discusses what a criminologist is, and considers the differences between a criminologist, a criminalist, and a criminal justice professional. Various professional opportunities for individuals with degrees in criminology are explored. The field of criminology itself is also discussed in detail, with various definitions considered. While criminology is primarily a social science, it is interdisciplinary. It contributes to, and overlaps, the field of criminal justice. One subfield is theoretical criminology, which posits explanations for criminal behavior. General and integrated theories of crime are compared.

The development of social policies based on research findings may be of broader importance to society than theory testing. For example, despite widespread concern among professional groups about the effect of the media on teenage violence, policymakers have been reluctant to curtail the production of violent media. Essentially, there is a conflict between crime reduction policies and the profit motives of media vendors. Concern over crime is one of the key issues in the country, making it an important determinant of public policy.

The social policy theme of the text is expanded through a contrast of the two main perspectives popular in today's society: the social problems perspective and the social responsibility perspective. Recently, the social responsibility perspective has had a substantial influence on national crime control policy.

Crime does not occur in a vacuum; every crime has a unique set of causes, consequences, and participants. Crime is seen as a social event rather than as an isolated individual activity. The criminal event is the result of the coming together of inputs provided by the offender, the victim, the criminal justice system, and the general public (society). Background and foreground features or inputs provided by each contributor are discussed. In addition, each crime has consequences, or outputs, which affect not only the victim and offender but also society and the criminal justice system. These consequences may be immediate or more long-term.

This text recognizes the primacy of sociology: the belief that the primary perspective from which many contemporary criminologists operate is a sociological one. However, not all criminologists agree with this perspective, and new and emerging perspectives are being developed.

Key Concepts

Crime: Human conduct in violation of the criminal laws of a state, the federal government, or a local jurisdiction that has the power to make such laws.

Criminal justice: The scientific study of crime, the criminal law, and components of the criminal justice system, including the police, courts, and corrections.

Criminal justice system: The various agencies of justice, especially the police, courts, and corrections, whose goal it is to apprehend, convict, punish, and rehabilitate law violators.

Criminalist: A specialist in the collection and examination of the physical evidence of crime.

Criminality: A behavioral predisposition that disproportionately favors criminal activity.

Criminalize: To make illegal.

Criminologist: One who is trained in the field of criminology. Also, one who studies crime, criminals, and criminal behavior.

Criminology: An interdisciplinary profession built around the scientific study of crime and criminal behavior, including their forms, causes, legal aspects, and control.

Deviant behavior: Human activity that violates social norms.

General theory: One that attempts to explain all (or at least most) forms of criminal conduct through a single, overarching approach.

Integrated theory: An explanatory perspective that merges (or attempts to merge) concepts drawn from different sources.

Social policy: A government initiative, program, or plan intended to address problems in society. The "war on crime," for example, is a kind of generic (large-scale) social policy—one consisting of many smaller programs.

Socialization: The lifelong process of social experience whereby individuals acquire the cultural patterns of their society.

Social problems perspective: The belief that crime is a manifestation of underlying social problems, such as poverty, discrimination, pervasive family violence, inadequate socialization practices, and the breakdown of traditional social institutions.

Social relativity: The notion that social events are differently interpreted according to the cultural experiences and personal interests of the initiator, the observer, or the recipient of that behavior.

Social responsibility perspective: The belief that individuals are fundamentally responsible for their own behavior and that they choose crime over other, more law-abiding courses of action.

Statute: A formal written enactment of a legislative body.

Statutory law: Law in the form of statutes or formal, written strictures made by a legislature or governing body with the power to make law.

Theory: A series of interrelated propositions that attempt to describe, explain, predict, and ultimately to control some class of events. A theory gains explanatory power from inherent logical consistency and is "tested" by how well it describes and predicts reality.

Unicausal: Having one cause. Unicausal theories posit only one source for all that they attempt to explain.

Questions for Review

1. What are the four definitional perspectives in contemporary criminology? What is the definition of *crime* that the authors of this textbook have chosen to use?
2. What is crime? What is the difference between crime and deviance? How might the notion of crime change over time? What impact does the changing nature of crime have on criminology?
3. What is the legalistic approach to the study of crime? How can it be used to decide what forms of behavior are criminal?
4. What do criminologists do? Provide a list of employment opportunities available in the field of criminology.
5. What are the various definitions of *criminology* presented in this chapter? Which is the one chosen by the authors of this textbook? Why?
6. How does contemporary criminology influence social policy? Do you think that policymakers should address crime as a matter of individual responsibility and accountability, or do you think that crime is truly a symptom of a dysfunctional society? Why?
7. What is the theme of this textbook? What are the differences between the social problems and the social responsibility perspectives on crime causation?
8. Describe the various participants in a criminal event. How does each contribute to an understanding of the event?
9. In what way is contemporary criminology interdisciplinary? Why is the sociological perspective especially important in studying crime? What other perspectives might be relevant? Why?

Questions for Reflection

1. This book emphasizes a social problems versus social responsibility theme. Describe both perspectives. How might social policy decisions based on these perspectives vary?
2. Do you think you might want to become a criminologist? Why or why not?
3. What do crimes such as doctor-assisted suicide tell us about the nature of the law and about crime in general? Do you believe that doctor-assisted suicide should be legalized? Why or why not?
4. Are there any crimes today that you think should be legalized? If so, what are they and why?
5. Can you think of any advances now occurring in the social or physical sciences that might soon have a significant impact on our understanding of crime and criminality? If so, what would those advances be? How might they impact our understanding of crime and criminal behavior?

Student Exercises

Activity #1

Watch a number of reality-based television shows such as *Cops* and keep a record of the following information for each crime/event:

1. The gender and race of the suspects
2. The gender and race of the police officers

3. The type of crime
4. The products being advertised during these programs

Questions to consider:

1. What is the predominant race of the suspects? The police officers?
2. Do you notice any difference in the behavior of the suspects and police officers when they are both of the same race? Of different races? Of different genders?
3. What types of crimes are featured? Does one type of crime predominate?
4. Are the products advertised during these programs directed toward any specific subgroup of the population? Are they age- or gender-based?

Activity #2

First, identify five behaviors that are against the law but which you do not consider to be deviant as well as five legal behaviors that you do consider to be deviant. Your instructor will divide the class into groups. Within each group, compare and contrast the items on your lists. Focus on the wide range of opinions present among a fairly homogenous group (university students studying criminal justice). Discuss possible reasons for differing opinions (for example, religious beliefs, profession, prior experiences with the criminal justice system).

Criminology Today on the Web

www.talkjustice.com/cybrary.asp

This site is maintained by the author of your textbook, Dr. Frank Schmalleger, and includes an extensive collection of links to criminal justice and criminology Web sites.

www.criminology.fsu.edu/cjlinks

This is Dr. Cecil Greek's Criminal Justice Links, which includes a huge number of links to all sorts of criminology and criminal justice Web sites.

http://faculty.ncwc.edu/toconnor/linklist.htm

This is the Criminal Justice Mega-Sites Web page, which includes an annotated list of criminology and criminal justice sites.

Student Study Guide Questions

True/False

_____ 1. The legalistic perspective defines *crime* as conduct in violation of the criminal law.

_____ 2. Formalized laws have always existed.

_____ 3. The political perspective defines *crime* in terms of popular notions of right and wrong.

_____ 4. The sociological perspective sees crime as encompassing any harmful acts.

_____ 5. A unified definition of *crime* is simple to achieve.

_____ 6. All criminal behavior is deviant.

_____ 7. The pluralistic perspective is most applicable to societies characterized by a shared belief system.

_____ 8. A shared consensus is easy to achieve in the United States.

_____ 9. There is a growing tendency to apply the term *criminologist* to anyone who works in the criminal justice field.

_____ 10. A judge is a criminalist.

_____ 11. Criminology is an interdisciplinary field.

_____ 12. Theoretical criminology focuses on describing crime and its occurrence.

_____ 13. Crime in the United States has been increasing for the past decade.

_____ 14. The social problems perspective is also known as the individual responsibility perspective.

_____ 15. According to the text, crime is an isolated individual activity.

_____ 16. Inputs are the background causes of crime.

_____ 17. Background contributions to crime are generally not very important.

_____ 18. Proper system response may increase crime.

Fill in the Blank

19. The _____ perspective sees crime as human conduct that violates the criminal law.

20. To criminalize a behavior involves making it _____.

21. The sociological perspective considers crime to be a(n) _____ act.

22. The psychological perspective is also known as the _____ perspective.

23. _____ is human behavior that violates social norms.

24. Societies with shared values, norms, and belief systems are best described by the _____ perspective.

25. A _____ specializes in the collection and examination of the physical evidence of crime.

26. Preliterate people appear to have explained deviant behavior by reference to _____.

27. The term *criminology* was coined by _____.

28. _____ is an interdisciplinary profession built around the scientific study of crime and criminal behavior.

29. In addition to being a field of study or a collection of theories, criminology is also a _____.

30. Criminology contributes to the discipline of _____.

31. A _____ theory posits a single, identifiable source for all criminal behavior.

32. The social problems perspective is characteristic of what social scientists term a _____ approach.

33. The social responsibility perspective is also known as the _____ responsibility perspective.

34. The immediate results or consequences of crime are known as _____.

35. A specific intent is an example of a _____ contribution to crime by the offender.

36. The primacy of sociology emphasizes that crime is a _____.

Multiple Choice

37. "Human conduct that is in violation of the criminal laws of a state, the federal government, or a local jurisdiction that has the power to make such laws" is a definition of
    a. criminology.
    b. crime.
    c. criminal.
    d. deviance.

38. The legalistic approach would suggest that crime is socially relative in the sense that it is created by
    a. legislative activity.
    b. social mores.
    c. the democratic process.
    d. human conduct.

39. The concept that crime is defined in terms of the power structures that exist in society exemplifies the _____ perspective.
    a. sociological
    b. mainstream
    c. political
    d. psychological

40. The belief that crime is an antisocial act of such a nature that repression is necessary to preserve the existing system of society is the basis of the _____ perspective on crime.
    a. legal
    b. political
    c. sociological
    d. psychological

41. The psychological perspective sees crime primarily as
    a. a violation of a law.
    b. an offense against human relationships.
    c. a form of social maladjustment.
    d. problem behavior.

42. Because you were late for this exam, you exceeded the speed limit by about 10 to 15 miles per hour while driving to class. This is an example of behavior that is
    a. deviant but not criminal.
    b. criminal but not deviant.
    c. both deviant and criminal.
    d. neither deviant nor criminal.

43. The gun-control debate is an example of the _____ perspective.
    a. consensus
    b. psychological
    c. sociological
    d. pluralistic

44. One who studies crime, criminals, and criminal behavior is called a
    a. scientist.
    b. criminal justice professional.
    c. criminologist.
    d. criminalism.

45. The official publication of the American Society of Criminology is
    a. *Criminology*.
    b. *Justice Quarterly*.
    c. *The Journal of Quantitative Criminology*.
    d. *Crime and Delinquency*.

46. The _____ definition of *criminology* literally defines the term as "the study of crime."
    a. linguistic
    b. disciplinary
    c. causative
    d. scientific

47. Which of the following is *not* one of the three principle components of criminology proposed by Clarence Ray Jeffery?
    a. Detection of the offender
    b. The control of crime
    c. Treatment
    d. Explanation of crime and criminal behavior

48. Which of the following is a disciplinary definition of *criminology*?
    a. Criminology is the body of knowledge regarding the social problem of crime.
    b. Criminology is the scientific study of crime.
    c. Criminology is the study of the causes of crime.
    d. Criminology is the scientific study of crime, criminals, and criminal behavior.

49. The field of study that is concerned primarily with the causes and consequences of crime is
    a. criminology.
    b. criminal justice.
    c. criminality.
    d. criminalistics.

50. A(n) _____ theory does not necessarily attempt to explain all criminality.
    a. general
    b. integrated
    c. unicausal
    d. complete

51. The social problems perspective holds that crime is
    a. a manifestation of underlying social problems.
    b. chosen by individual perpetrators.
    c. not going to be solved by social programs.
    d. none of the above

52. Which of the following crime reduction or prevention strategies is most characteristic of the social problems perspective?
    a. A government-funded initiative to enhance educational opportunities among low-income individuals
    b. A move to broaden police powers by increasing the number of exceptions to the Exclusionary Rule
    c. Rewriting state statutes to increase the severity of punishment for violent offenders, such as three-strikes laws
    d. All of the above

53. Which of the following is not a foreground contribution by an offender?
    a. A particular motivation
    b. A peculiar biology
    c. A specific intent
    d. A drug-induced state of mind

54. A victim may actively contribute to his/her own victimization through the appearance of
    a. defensiveness.
    b. exposure.
    c. defenselessness.
    d. precipitation.

Word Search Puzzle

```
G E L O F B K L H U E J B H P R O D U Y A W S N Z
R T Y U L C X V X E L I F H C J I N Y D D Z B Z N
J U V Y M Z K V J A X V F F D U T B A P T D G P L
I Q R Q S V U P U Y X Z L Z I J Q B D P L J P W L
L D Q H G R V N Z S V Q A B P U N I C A U S A L D
W H C O I W T Q E B J Q P W M A W G C T L T D T U
Q X R X L S Z Y R K H S F E Q B R U H W F E U T R
U D I Y Y G X Z M J I T V Y Q A M Z S Z Q E R O X
J I M K I B G I W C M X S T A T U T E L S O B U B
V N I Z Z G H G H R N A Y Q V M I M L K C H R G C
P T N K D R Q C P I K B E B H D E V I A N T H U R
W E O S Q F M R N M E T S F J S B U K Q C P L Q I
C G L T U T F I U I H S A M L A I S C A Y K H H M
R R O X G V I M K N T S P B G H V L G D U W Y R I
I A G R K Y E E Y O F L F C R I M I N A L I T Y N
M T I G I R K B A L K B J O R K H V V Q O L N B A
I E S K A Y G Z S O F I W D G U P O Q U C I Q M L
N D T Y R G O L N G O R V B H K B C B V U W Y U I
A Z N Z C X N I W Y D X Y R B Q Q T D F W S T U S
L A C B Z D V E W O Z F W Y T U B P K M N G E T T
I N M K H Y Q U Y Y E T S O C I A L I Z A T I O N
Z P W J Q H L U H J P I A A Y Y T H E O R Y Q U L
E L Z Q R C D I B Q Y L Z F N B C L O B E D I X H
J W B O Y Y N Q Z W A H T J Y I E J D N U T P U F
B S K I K E K Q F E S U W V O K O M C P R R D Y R
```

Crime	Criminalist	Criminality	Criminalize	Criminologist	Criminology
Integrated	Socialization	Statute	Theory	Unicausal	Deviant

Crossword Puzzle

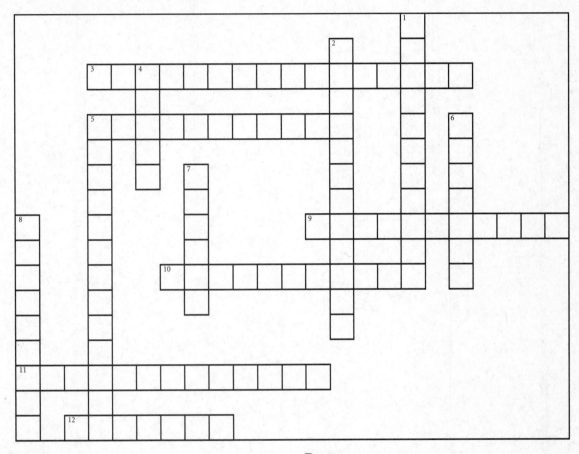

Across

3. The notion that social events are differently interpreted according to cultural experiences and personal interests (two words).

5. A specialist in the collection and examination of the physical evidence of crime.

9. To make illegal.

10. An interdisciplinary profession built around the scientific study of crime.

11. The process of social experience by which individuals acquire cultural patterns.

12. A formal written enactment of a legislative body.

Down

1. A behavioral predisposition that disproportionately favors criminal activity.

2. Law in the form of formal written strictures (two words).

4. Human conduct in violation of the criminal laws of a state, the federal government, or a local jurisdiction that has the power to make such laws.

5. One who studies crime, criminals, and criminal behavior.

6. Human activity that violates social norms.

7. A series of interrelated propositions that describe, explain, predict, and control events.

8. Having one cause.

2 Patterns of Crime

Learning Outcomes

After reading this chapter, students should be able to:

- Explain the history of statistical crime data collection and analysis and understand the usefulness and limitations of crime data
- Recognize the various methods currently used to collect and disseminate crime data
- Describe the three major shifts in crime rates since record keeping began, and identify the likely direction of coming changes in such rates
- Describe the nature of the crime problem in America today, and explain how we can assess its extent
- List the major crimes on which data is gathered, and describe the extent of each
- Provide an overview of the FBI's Part II offenses, and describe the extent of such crimes
- Describe sources of crime data that are available in the United States in addition to FBI and NCVS statistics
- Discuss how criminologists gather information on unreported crimes, and explain what is meant by the "dark figure of crime"
- Define and discuss the social dimensions of crime, including key demographic factors

Chapter Outline

Chapter Summary

This chapter describes various sources of crime statistics. It begins with a brief history of crime statistics, focusing on Thomas Robert Malthus, Adolphe Quételet, and André Michel Guerry, and reviewing the developing of the statistical school of criminology.

The two primary sources of information on crime in the United States today are official statistics and victimization statistics. Official statistics are found in the FBI's *Uniform Crime Reports* (UCR) and National Incident-Based Reporting System (NIBRS). Both are compiled annually by the FBI and contain data provided by police departments around the country. However, official statistics only include information on crimes known to the police and provide no insight into the dark figure of unreported crime. Victimization statistics, as provided by the National Crime Victimization Survey (NCVS), seek to obtain information on unreported crime. Subjects in the survey are asked about their victimization experiences; information is collected on the crime, the offender, and the specific incident, including whether or not the victim reported the criminal event to the police. Both sources of information have limitations. The differences among the three sources are reviewed.

There have been three major shifts in crime rates since official crime statistics were first gathered. The first occurred during the early 1940s, due to the outbreak of World War II, when crime decreased significantly. The second shift, a dramatic increase in crime, began in the 1960s and ended in the 1990s. A number of factors contributed to this increase, including the entry of baby boomers into their teenage "crime-prone" years, modified reporting practices that resulting in increased reporting of crime, and the tumult of the 1960s. The third shift, a decrease in crime, began in the mid-1990s and was due in great part to economic and demographic factors.

Because official statistics are limited, some researchers suggest that the size of the correctional population might provide a more accurate picture of the crime problem in the United States than the crime rate. It is also clear that, despite the fact that crime rates appear to be decreasing, they are still much higher than those in most other industrialized nations. Elliott Currie proposes the use of a criminality index, which is the sum of the actual crime rate and the latent crime rate (based on crimes that would be committed by offenders incapacitated by the criminal justice system). Calculations based on this index reveal a crime problem that is significantly higher than that suggested by official statistics.

The text also discusses the eight Part I or index offenses defined by the UCR. These include criminal homicide, forcible rape, robbery, aggravated assault, burglary, larceny, motor vehicle theft, and arson. Information about these crimes obtained from the UCR and the NCVS is presented. Hate crimes and Part II crimes are also discussed.

Information on unreported crime, known as the "dark figure of crime," also may be obtained from self-report surveys, in which anonymous respondents are asked to report confidentially any crimes they may have committed. The best known such surveys include the National Youth Survey, which surveys juveniles between the ages of 11 and 17, and the Monitoring the Future study, which focuses on the behaviors, attitudes, and values of students and young adults in the United States.

The social dimensions of crime are aspects of crime and victimization as they relate to socially significant attributes by which groups are defined and according to which individuals are assigned group membership. These include age, gender, ethnicity or race, and social class or standing in society. Criminal activity is associated more with youth, and most forms of criminality decrease with age (the desistance phenomenon). Elderly offenders are more likely to commit crimes requiring special skills and knowledge. The elderly are less likely to be victimized than any other group. Gender may be the best single predictor of criminality, with males being much more likely than women to commit most crimes. Women are also victimized less frequently than men in most crime categories (with the exceptions of the crimes of rape and spouse abuse).

Race may also be related to crime; arrest rates of blacks are significantly higher than their proportion in the population. The question of whether the criminal justice system is racist is discussed. Blacks are also more likely to be victimized than whites; the high rates of both crime and criminal victimization within the black community have led to a heightened fear of crime among blacks in the United States. The relationship of social class to crime originally assumed to exist began to be questioned in the 1960s. Recent data from the National Youth Survey does suggest that a fairly significant correlation between criminality and social class exists, with members of lower social classes being more likely to be involved in serious street crimes.

Key Concepts

Aggravated assault: An unlawful attack by one person upon another for the purpose of inflicting severe or aggravated bodily injury. (UCR definition)

Arson: Any willful or malicious burning or attempt to burn, with or without intent to defraud, a dwelling house, public building, motor vehicle or aircraft, personal property of another, and so on.

Burglary: By the narrowest and oldest definition: the trespassory breaking and entering of the dwelling house of another in the nighttime with the intent to commit a felony. Also, the unlawful entry of a structure to commit a felony or a theft. The UCR definition of *burglary* is the unlawful entry of any fixed structure, vehicle, or vessel used for regular residence, industry, or business, with or without force, with intent to commit a felony or larceny.

Carjacking: The stealing of a car while it is occupied.

Clearance rate: The proportion of reported or discovered crimes within a given offense category that are solved.

Cohort: A group of individuals having certain significant social characteristics in common, such as gender and date and place of birth.

Correlation: A causal, complementary, or reciprocal relationship between two measurable variables.

Criminal homicide: The illegal killing of one human being by another. Also, the UCR category that includes and is limited to all offenses of causing the death of another person without justification or excuse.

Criminality index: The actual extent of the crime problem in a society. The criminality index is computed by adding the actual crime rate and the latent crime rate.

Dark figure of crime: The numerical total of unreported crimes that are not reflected in official crime statistics.

Date rape: Unlawful forced sexual intercourse with a woman against her will that occurs within the context of a dating relationship.

Demographics: The characteristics of population groups, usually expressed in statistical fashion.

Desistance phenomenon: The observable decrease in crime rates that is invariably associated with age.

Felony murder: A special class of criminal homicide in which an offender may be charged with first-degree murder when that person's criminal activity results in another person's death.

First-degree murder: Criminal homicide that is planned or involves premeditation.

Forcible rape: The carnal knowledge of a female forcibly and against her will. Assaults or attempts to commit rape by force or threat of force are also included in the UCR definition; however, statutory rape (without force) and other sex offenses are excluded.

Hate crime: A criminal offense in which the motive is hatred, bias, or prejudice, based on the actual or perceived race, color, religion, national origin, ethnicity, gender, or sexual orientation of another individual or group of individuals. Also called *bias crime*.

Larceny-theft: *Larceny* is defined as the unlawful taking or attempted taking of property (other than a motor vehicle) from the possession of another, by stealth, without force or deceit, with intent to permanently deprive the owner of the property. The UCR definition of *larceny-theft* is the unlawful taking, carrying, leading, or riding away of property (other than a motor vehicle) from the possession or constructive possession of another. Attempts are included.

Latent crime rate: A rate of crime calculated on the basis of crimes that would likely be committed by those who are in prison or jail or who are otherwise incapacitated by the justice system.

Monitoring the Future: A national self-report survey on drug use that has been conducted since 1975.

Motor vehicle theft: As defined by the UCR, the theft or attempted theft of a motor vehicle. According to the Federal Bureau of Investigation, this offense category includes the stealing of automobiles, trucks, buses, motorcycles, motorscooters, and snowmobiles.

National Crime Victimization Survey (NCVS):   A survey conducted annually by the Bureau of Justice Statistics that provides data on surveyed households that report they were affected by crime.

National Incident-Based Reporting System (NIBRS):   A new and enhanced statistical reporting system that will collect data on each single incident and arrest within 22 crime categories.

National Youth Survey (NYS):   A longitudinal panel study of a national sample of 1,725 individuals that measured self-reports of delinquency and other types of behavior.

Negligent homicide: The act of causing the death of another person by recklessness or gross negligence.

Part I offenses: The crimes of murder, rape, robbery, aggravated assault, burglary, larceny, and motor vehicle theft, as defined under the FBI's Uniform Crime Reporting Program. Also called *major crimes*.

Part II offenses: Less serious offenses as identified by the FBI for the purpose of reporting arrest data.

Rape: As defined by the NCVS, carnal knowledge through the use of force or the threat of force, including attempts. Statutory rape (without force) is excluded. Both heterosexual and homosexual rape are included. For the UCR definition, see **forcible rape.**

Robbery: The taking or attempting to take anything of value from the care, custody, or control of a person or persons by force or threat of force or violence or by putting the victim in fear. (UCR definition)

Second-degree murder: Criminal homicide that is unplanned and is often described as a "crime of passion."

Self-report survey: A survey in which anonymous respondents, without fear of disclosure or arrest, are asked to confidentially report any violations of the criminal law that they have committed.

Simple assault: An attack without a weapon, resulting either in minor injury or in undetermined injury requiring less than two days of hospitalization. (NCVS definition)

Spousal rape: The rape of one spouse by the other. The term usually refers to the rape of a woman by her husband.

Statistical school: A criminological perspective with roots in the early 1800s that seeks to uncover correlations between crime rates and other types of demographic data.

Uniform Crime Reporting (UCR) Program: A Federal Bureau of Investigation summation of crime statistics tallied annually and consisting primarily of data on crimes reported to the police and of arrests.

Questions for Review

1. How did the gathering of crime data begin in the United States? How has it evolved since that time?
2. What are the major differences among the NCVS and UCR/NIBRS? Can useful comparisons be made between these two programs? If so, what kinds of comparisons might be made?
3. What major shifts in crime rates have occurred since record keeping began in the United States? What future direction are crime rates likely to take?
4. What is the nature of the crime problem in the United States today? How can we best measure it?
5. What are the major crimes on which data is gathered today? How prevalent is each?
6. How do Part II offenses, reported by the FBI, differ from Part I offenses? How common are Part II crimes today?
7. What are the major available sources of contemporary crime data in the United States? What other sources exist?
8. What resources and techniques exist for gathering information about crimes that are not reported to the police? What is the "dark figure of crime"?
9. What is meant by the "social dimensions of crime"? Which social dimensions does this chapter discuss?

Questions for Reflection

1. This book emphasizes a social problems versus a social responsibility theme. Which perspective is best supported by a realistic appraisal of the "social dimensions" of crime discussed in this chapter? Explain.

2. This chapter says that African Americans appear to be overrepresented in many categories of criminal activity. Do you believe that the statistics cited in this chapter accurately reflect the degree of black and white involvement in crime? Why? How might those statistics be inaccurate?

3. What does it mean to say that the traditional UCR was summary-based, while the newer NIBRS is incident-based? When NIBRS is fully operational, what kinds of data will it contribute to the UCR Program? How will this information be useful?

4. What is a crime rate? How are rates useful? How might the NCVS and the UCR/NIBRS make better use of rates?

5. Why don't victims report crimes to the police? Which crimes appear to be the least frequently reported? Why are those crimes so rarely reported? Which crimes appear to be the most frequently reported? Why are they so often reported?

Student Exercises

Activity #1

This activity involves comparing the definitions used by the FBI with those used by state criminal codes.

1. Obtain the definitions used by the FBI for each of the eight Part I offenses. This information is available on the World Wide Web at the FBI's Web site (www.fbi.gov/ucr/ucr.htm).

2. Obtain the definitions of the same eight crimes for your state. One way to locate state statutes on the Web is to access the Cornell University School of Law's Legal Information Institute Web site at www.law.cornell.edu/states/listing.html. (**Note:** Your instructor may choose to assign you a different state.)

3. Compare and contrast the definitions used by the FBI with those of your state. What differences do you see?

Activity #2

Your instructor will assign you two large cities in the United States and one index offense (for example, burglary). Go to the FBI's Web site and access the most recent UCR data for these two cities. Answer the following questions:

1. How many burglaries occurred in each city (attach printouts from the UCR showing burglary counts)?

2. Which city had more reported burglaries?

3. What were the burglary rates for each of the two cities?

4. Did the burglary rates change over time in either city?

5. What factors might explain the differences in the burglary rates?

Criminology Today on the Web

www.fbi.gov/ucr/ucr.htm

This Web site will provide you with access to recent issues of the *Uniform Crime Reports* as well as information on the National Incident-Based Reporting System and other statistics collected by the FBI.

www.ojp.usdoj.gov/bjs

This is the home page for the Bureau of Justice Statistics. From here you can access recent issues of the *National Crime Victimization Survey* as well as data from many other sources.

www.albany.edu/sourcebook

This Web site provides a link to the *Sourcebook of Criminal Justice Statistics*, which is supported by the Bureau of Justice Statistics and includes data from many sources covering many aspects of the U.S. criminal justice system. The *Sourcebook* is only available in electronic format.

www.law.cornell.edu

This is the site of the Legal Information Institute of the Cornell University School of Law. It includes links to federal and state constitutions, statutes, and codes of law.

Student Study Guide Questions

True/False

_____ 1. The collection of population statistics is a relatively new phenomenon.

_____ 2. If an offender is deceased, the crime cannot be cleared.

_____ 3. NIBRS is fully implemented.

_____ 4. Hate crimes are most commonly perpetrated against an individual.

_____ 5. The NCVS began collecting data in 1929.

_____ 6. Households remain in the NCVS sample for as long as they wish to participate.

_____ 7. Second-degree murder involves the concept of malice aforethought.

_____ 8. Most murder offenders are male.

_____ 9. A recent study of rape found that rape of young girls is rare.

_____ 10. Higher income families are more likely to be robbed.

_____ 11. According to the UCR, aggravated assaults are more common in the summer months.

_____ 12. According to the UCR definition, the use of force to gain entry is essential to classify an offense as burglary.

_____ 13. Self-report surveys provide information on the dark figure of crime.

_____ 14. Fear of future victimization is one of the most common reasons for not reporting a violent victimization to the police.

_____ 15. When one variable increases in value as another decreases, a negative correlation exists.

_____ 16. Criminal activity is more associated with youth than with any other stage of life.

_____ 17. The elderly are more likely to be victimized than other groups.

_____ 18. According to the NCVS, black women aged 65 or older have the lowest violent crime victimization rates.

Fill in the Blank

19. The English economist _____ described a worldwide future of warfare, crime, and starvation.

20. According to Adolphe Quételet, property crime rates _____ during the colder months of the year.

21. A crime is considered to be _____ when an arrest has been made or when the perpetrator is known but an arrest is not possible.

22. Unreported criminal activity is known as the _____.

23. The Hate Crime Statistics Act of 1990 requires the _____ to collect and report data on hate crimes.

24. According to the NCVS, approximately _____ of all violent crimes are reported to the police.

25. _____ is the willful killing of one human being by another.

26. _____ has the highest clearance rate of any index offense.

27. Scholars such as A. Nicholas Groth consider rape to be a crime of _____.

28. A _____ robbery refers to a robbery where the offender was unarmed.

29. According to the UCR, the rate of burglary has been _____ during the 1990s.

30. The _____ established campus crime statistic reporting requirements for universities receiving any form of federal funding.

31. According to the NCVS, as the value of property loss increases, the likelihood that a household crime will be reported _____.

32. _____ are more likely to report violent victimizations to the police.

33. Race and income are examples of _____ attributes.

34. A(n) _____ is a connection or association observed to exist between two measurable variables.

35. The arrest rate for murder among African Americans is _____ times that for whites.

36. Prior to 1960, criminologists assumed that a _____ existed between social class and crime.

Multiple Choice

37. The thermic law of crime was developed by
    a. André Michel Guerry.
    b. Cesare Beccaria.
    c. Adolphe Quételet.
    d. Thomas Robert Malthus.

38. The *Sourcebook of Criminal Justice Statistics* contains data from the
    a. Uniform Crime Reporting Program.
    b. National Crime Victimization Survey.
    c. National Incident-Based Reporting System.
    d. all of the above

39. Which of the following is *not* a UCR Part I offense?
    a. Arson
    b. Fraud
    c. Burglary
    d. Theft of a motor vehicle

40. UCR Part I offenses are subdivided into two categories:
    a. felonies and misdemeanors.
    b. violent crimes and personal crimes.
    c. violent personal crimes and property crimes.
    d. violent personal crimes and index crimes.

41. Hate crimes are most commonly committed by
    a. black males.
    b. black females.
    c. white males.
    d. white females.

42. According to the NCVS, members of which racial group experience the highest rates of violent victimization?
    a. Whites
    b. African Americans
    c. Hispanics
    d. Asians

43. Based on NCVS findings, which of the following individuals would be most likely to be the victim of a violent crime?

    a. A young black male
    b. A young black female
    c. A young white male
    d. A young white female

44. Which of the following was *not* a possible cause of the increase in reported crime between the 1960s and the 1990s?

    a. Victims becoming sensitized to the importance of reporting crimes
    b. More accurate and increased data collection by police departments
    c. The disruption and tumult of the 1960s
    d. The aging out of the baby-boom generation

45. Official crime rates in the United States are _____; correctional populations are _____.

    a. decreasing; increasing
    b. decreasing; decreasing
    c. increasing, decreasing
    d. increasing; increasing

46. _____ is legally seen as a true crime of passion.

    a. First-degree murder
    b. Second-degree murder
    c. Third-degree murder
    d. Negligent homicide

47. According to the UCR, the rate of reported forcible rape is highest in the _____ months.

    a. summer
    b. spring
    c. winter
    d. fall

48. Robbery that occurs in a public place, generally out of doors, is known as _____ robbery.

    a. strong-arm
    b. armed
    c. highway
    d. simple

49. If you unlawfully enter a structure to commit a felony, you have probably committed the crime of

    a. theft.
    b. robbery.
    c. burglary.
    d. breaking and entering.

50. According to UCR larceny statistics, most items reported stolen were taken from
    a. buildings.
    b. coin-operated machines.
    c. motor vehicles.
    d. private residences.

51. According to the UCR, most motor vehicle thefts occur in
    a. large cities.
    b. small cities.
    c. suburbs.
    d. rural areas.

52. Vanity pyromaniacs commit arson because they
    a. suffer from psychological problems.
    b. are trying to take credit for putting out the fire they originally started.
    c. are trying to defraud an insurance company.
    d. are attempting to disguise another felony, such as burglary or murder.

53. Which of the following is *not* a UCR Part II offense?
    a. Simple assault
    b. Aggravated assault
    c. Fraud
    d. Gambling

54. *The Myth of a Racist Criminal Justice System* was written by
    a. Marvin D. Free, Jr.
    b. William Wilbanks.
    c. James Fox.
    d. Coramae Richey Mann.

Word Search Puzzle

```
E C K V L A R C E N Y S J N D W M Y M H W C E M X
K W B G O P E U A D D E S I S T A N C E B P R Q V
J G U C Q R M G E W Q O U W I L S O N O Y V I M F
F C K E O T C S I R E L O M V T X L B R C K W C W
Y J K W Y Y N H X Y N R L U O U F L W D O W W J U
R T E N C V S B D Q G D A F R A O U F E F W U Z X
I X O A R D L M N X V R U W S F N M L M A Q Q K G
N C O R R E L A T I O N P D T M I W B O B U B V X
J T F L S D Q O S S E V U U Z L W B L G H E R J M
Q I U Q E N N K B R N C P P P P Y V U R N T A M P
Z M E J L O V S O Y R M U R D E R A M A E E I B I
M Y V W F D A R K F I G U R E F C D S P E L T Q W
W A B W R P T E L P Q Q S J Z E W M T H B E H L E
D R U H E C S C A Y L J D C T R S H E I J T W I C
A S R P P O B C O H O R T R W U C O I C R Q A V D
T O G R O A W I R G Z N G S N O Y M N S P U I P V
E N L H R Y Q F C W V Q P A P U J I Q B W I T Y L
R G A A T T R Q E Y Y F F X Z F J C B C I C E J A
A H R T C D N B J G Q Y E J S N K I Z Z L Y C J X
P X Y E N V A X R O B B E R Y S K D Z L B Y N V L
E Y R C L O F D A C W R A K B L O E S R A X M I K
S Q V R X N I B R S P E T E R S I L I A N N O G E
Y H A I M A U E R F A O D H C A R J A C K I N G L
G V T M I R C Z S L G N P K J W N G L A S I D K V
V B C E P Z D V Q U R A P E O Y H K Z V V P A V M
```

Arson	Blumstein	Braithwaite	Burglary	Carjacking	Cohort
Correlation	Dark figure	Date rape	Demographics	Desistance	Hate crime
Homicide	Larceny	Murder	NCVS	NIBRS	Petersilia
Quetelet	Rape	Robbery	Self report	Wilbanks	Wilson

Crossword Puzzle

Across

1. A group of individuals having certain significant social characteristics in common.
3. The observable decrease in crime rates associated with age.
5. Carnal knowledge through the use of force or the threat of force.
6. Stealing a car while it is occupied.
9. A relationship between two measurable variables.
11. Taking something of value from another person by force.
12. A crime motivated by bias based on the victim's perceived race, color, religion, sexual orientation, etc. (two words).
13. A victim survey conducted annually by the Bureau of Justice Statistics.
14. The rape of a woman by her husband (two words).

Down

1. The proportion of reported or discovered crimes that are solved (two words).
2. A new statistical reporting system that collects data on every incident and arrest.
3. The characteristics of population groups.
4. The unlawful entry of a structure with intent to commit a felony or theft.
7. The willful or malicious burning of a building or personal property of another.
8. The number of unreported crimes that are not reflected in official crime statistics (two words).
10. Illegally taking the property of another without force.

3 Where Do Theories Come From?

Learning Outcomes

After reading this chapter, students should be able to:

- Recognize the role of criminological research in theory development, and display an understanding of various types of research designs
- Appreciate the relevance of criminological theory to the study of crime and criminals
- Discuss the role of research and experimentation in theory building
- Explain the differences between quantitative and qualitative methods in the social sciences
- Recognize the ethical considerations involved in conducting criminological research
- Identify the impact of criminological research and experimental criminology on the creation of social policy
- Describe the process of writing a research report and identify common sources for publishing research findings

Chapter Outline

Chapter Summary

Criminological theory cannot be fully appreciated unless one understands its fundamental assumptions. This chapter examines how social scientific research methods are used in the development of criminological theories. A theory is a series of interrelated propositions that attempt to describe, explain, predict, and ultimately control some class of events, such as criminal behavior. Theories serve a variety of purposes and are tested through research, the use of standardized, systematic procedures in the search for knowledge. Research can be pure or applied, and can be primary or secondary. Research is conducted in four stages: problem solving, research design development, the selection of data-gathering techniques, and a review of the findings. Experimental criminology uses social science techniques in theory testing and is helping to produce a growing body of evidence-based findings.

Problem identification involves choosing a problem or issue to be studied. The majority of criminological research is intended to explore causality issues, especially the claims made by theories that purport to explain criminal behavior. Much contemporary criminological research involves hypothesis testing. Research designs structure the research process. One basic design is the one-group pretest–post-test. However, this type of design does not eliminate the possibility of confounding effects, or rival explanations, which may affect both the internal and external validity of the research. The chapter lists a number of factors that may threaten the internal or external validity of a research design. The use of a controlled experiment or a quasi-experimental design may increase the validity of the results by eliminating some rival explanations. These designs require the use of randomization when assigning research subjects to experimental and control groups.

There are five main data-gathering strategies commonly used in criminology: survey research, case studies, participant observation, self-reporting, and secondary analysis. The strategy selected must produce information in a form usable to the researcher and thus depends on the questions to be answered. Data collection involves scientific observation, which must meet the criteria of intersubjectivity and replicability. Even so, some observations may lead to unwarranted conclusions. Once the data have been collected, they are usually analyzed in some way, generally using statistical techniques. Descriptive statistics, such as the mean, median, mode, and standard deviation, describe, summarize, and highlight the relationships within the data. Inferential statistics, including tests of significance, attempt to generalize findings by specifying how likely they are to be true for other populations or locations.

Research methods can be quantitative or qualitative. Both are useful and provide important information. Some criminologists believe that qualitative data-gathering strategies represent the future of criminological research.

Research is not conducted in a vacuum and cannot be free of biases and preconceptions. The best way to control biases is to be aware of them at the start of the research. Ethical issues are also extremely important; although they may not affect the validity of the results, they may have a significant impact upon the lives of researchers and subjects. Key ethical issues include protection of subjects from harm, privacy, disclosure, and data confidentiality. One way to overcome many of these ethical issues is through the use of informed consent. Criminological research may also have an impact on social policy, although many publicly elected officials may prefer to create politically expedient policies rather than consider current research.

After a research study has been conducted, the results usually are presented in the form of a research report or paper. There is a standard format that is generally followed. Most criminologists seek to publish their research results. The primary medium for such publication is refereed professional journals, which use peer reviewers to determine the quality of submitted manuscripts.

Key Concepts

Applied research: Scientific inquiry that is designed and carried out with practical applications in mind.

Confounding effects: A rival explanation, or competing hypothesis, that is a threat to the internal or external validity of a research design.

Control group: A group of experimental subjects that, although the subject of measurement and observation, is not exposed to the experimental intervention.

Controlled experiment: An experiment that attempts to hold conditions (other than the intentionally introduced experimental intervention) constant.

Data confidentiality: The ethical requirement of social scientific research to protect the confidentiality of individual research participants, while simultaneously preserving justified research access to the information participants provide.

Descriptive statistics: Statistics that describe, summarize, or highlight the relationships within data that have been gathered.

Evidence-based: That which is built on scientific findings; and especially practices and policies founded upon the results of randomized controlled experiments.

Experimental criminology: A form of contemporary criminology that makes use of rigorous social scientific techniques, especially randomized controlled experiments and the systematic review of research results.

External validity: The ability to generalize research findings to other settings.

Hypothesis: An explanation that accounts for a set of facts and that can be tested by further investigation. Also, something that is taken to be true for the purpose of argument or investigation.

Inferential statistics: Statistics that specify how likely findings are to be true for other populations or in other locales.

Informed consent: The ethical requirement of social scientific research that research subjects be informed as to the nature of the research about to be conducted, their anticipated role in it, and the uses to which the data they provide will be put.

Internal validity: The certainty that experimental interventions did indeed cause the changes observed in the study group. Also, the control over confounding factors that tend to invalidate the results of an experiment.

Intersubjectivity: A scientific principle that requires independent observers to see the same thing under the same circumstances for observations to be regarded as valid.

Meta-analysis: A study of other studies about a particular topic of interest.

Operationalization: The process by which concepts are made measurable.

Participant observation: A strategy in data gathering in which the researcher observes a group by participating, to varying degrees, in the activities of the group.

Primary research: Research characterized by original and direct investigation.

Pure research: Research undertaken simply for the sake of advancing scientific knowledge.

Qualitative method: A research technique that produces subjective results, or results that are difficult to quantify.

Quantitative method: A research technique that produces measurable results.

Quasi-experimental design: An approach to research that, although less powerful than experimental designs, is deemed worthy of use when better designs are not feasible.

Randomization: The process whereby individuals are assigned to study groups without biases or differences resulting from selection.

Replicability: A scientific principle in which valid observations made at one time can be made again at a later time if all other conditions are the same.

Research: The use of standardized, systematic procedures in the search for knowledge.

Research design: The logic and structure inherent in an approach to data gathering.

Secondary research: New evaluations of existing information that had been collected by other researchers.

Survey research: A social science data-gathering technique that involves the use of questionnaires.

Test of significance: A statistical technique intended to provide researchers with confidence that their results are, in fact, true and not the result of sampling error.

Theory: A series of interrelated propositions that attempt to describe, explain, predict, and ultimately to control some class of events. A theory gains explanatory power from inherent logical consistency and is "tested" by how well it describes and predicts reality.

Variable: A concept that can undergo measurable changes.

Verstehen: The kind of subjective understanding that can be achieved by criminologists who immerse themselves in the everyday world of the criminals they study.

Questions for Review

1. What is the role of criminological research in theory building?
2. How can theories help us to understand criminal behavior? To design strategies intended to control such behavior?
3. What role do research and experimentation play in theory building in criminology? How might a good research design be diagrammed? What kinds of threats to the validity of research designs can you identify? How can such threats be controlled or eliminated?
4. What are the differences between quantitative and qualitative methods in the social sciences? What are the advantages and disadvantages of each method?
5. What are some of the ethical considerations involved in conducting criminological research? How can researchers make sure that such considerations are met?
6. How do criminological research and experimental criminology impact social policy?
7. What sections might a typical research report contain? Where are research findings in criminology published?

Questions for Reflection

1. This book emphasizes a social problems versus social responsibility theme. How might a thorough research agenda allow us to decide which perspective is most fruitful in combating crime?
2. What is a hypothesis? What does it mean to operationalize a hypothesis? Why is operationalization necessary?
3. What is a theory? Why is the task of criminological theory construction so demanding? How do we know if a theory is any good?
4. What is a meta-analysis? For what purposes might a meta-analysis be conducted?

5. List and describe the various types of data-gathering strategies discussed in this chapter. Is any one technique "better" than another? Why? Under what kinds of conditions might certain types of data-gathering strategies be most appropriate?

6. In 2007, the Bureau of Justice Statistics announced its finding that male military veterans were less than half as likely as nonveteran men of the same age to be in prison (the rates reported were 630 versus 1,390 per 100,000 male prisoners, respectively). Does this mean that we can say with confidence that military service decreases a man's likelihood of committing a criminal offense? What other influences might be operating to lower the likelihood of crime commission by military veterans? (See the full BJS report at www.justicestudies.com/pubs/veterans.pdf.)

Student Exercises

Activity #1

Many social science organizations have adopted official codes of ethics. This exercise deals with the similarities and differences found in the ethical codes of various fields.

1. First, go to the Academy of Criminal Justice Sciences (ACJS) home page at www.acjs.org and access the code of ethics. What (if anything) does the ACJS code of ethics have to say about each of the following?
    - ➤ Informed consent
    - ➤ Confidentiality
    - ➤ Reporting of research
    - ➤ Protection of subjects from harm
    - ➤ Plagiarism
2. Then go to the home page of the American Sociological Association (ASA) at www.asanet.org and locate the ASA code of ethics. What does this code have to say about the subjects above?
3. Finally, go to the Web site of the American Psychological Association (APA) at www.apa.org/ethics and examine the APA code of ethics. What does this code have to say about the subjects above?
4. Which of the three codes do you prefer, and why?

Activity #2

Aprilville, a small town outside Bigcity, plans to implement a neighborhood watch program. The town mayor has asked you to find out if the program, once implemented, will have any effect on the town's crime rate. Design a research study to answer this question:

1. Formulate one or more hypotheses and operationalize the concepts.
2. Choose a research design from those discussed in the chapter and explain why you selected this design.
3. Select a data-gathering strategy and explain why you chose this technique.

Criminology Today on the Web

www.acjs.org

This is the home page for the Academy of Criminal Justice Sciences, an international organization that promotes scholarly and professional activities in criminal justice.

www.asc41.com

This is the home page for the American Society of Criminology, an international organization that promotes research, study, and educational activities in the field of criminology.

www.britsoccrim.org

This is the home page for the British Society of Criminology, the major criminological society of Great Britain. It includes the BSC code of ethics for researchers in the field of criminology.

http://arapaho.nsuok.edu/~dreveskr/CJRR.html-ssi

This site contains links to information about research methods and statistics in criminology.

Student Study Guide Questions

True/False

_____ 1. Armchair criminologists emphasize the use of research methods.

_____ 2. Research involves the use of standardized, systematic procedures in the search for knowledge.

_____ 3. Primary research is characterized by original and direct investigation.

_____ 4. A hypothesis cannot be tested until the concepts are operationalized.

_____ 5. In a one-group pretest–post-test design, the post-test involves observations made prior to the experimental intervention.

_____ 6. Confounding effects increase the certainty of results of any single series of observations.

_____ 7. Interviewer fatigue is an example of experimental mortality.

_____ 8. The reactive effects of testing are a threat to external validity.

_____ 9. A controlled experiment provides some control over factors that threaten external validity.

_____ 10. Reports generated out of the NCVS are the result of survey data.

_____ 11. Life histories may only be gathered on single subjects, not on groups of individuals.

_____ 12. A researcher using the participant as observer strategy does not have to be concerned about influencing the behavior of the group being observed.

_____ 13. Self-report studies are often a form of survey research.

_____ 14. If one variable increases whenever another does the same, a positive correlation exists.

_____ 15. The findings of qualitative methods are expressed numerically.

_____ 16. *Verstehen* relates to quantitative methodology.

_____ 17. Criminological research findings are frequently at odds with public sentiment.

_____ 18. A researcher may submit an article to several journals at the same time.

Fill in the Blank

19. A _____ is a set of interrelated propositions that provide a relatively complete form of understanding.

20. Theories provide _____ for the interpretation of data.

21. Theories supply _____ within which concepts and variables acquire special significance.

22. In _____ research, the research is working toward some practical goal.

23. A(n) _____ is something that is taken to be true for the purpose of argument or investigation.

24. Rival explanations or competing hypotheses are known as _____.

25. A threat to _____ validity reduces the researcher's confidence that the intervention will be as effective in the field as under laboratory-like conditions.

26. _____ involves events that occur between the first and second observations and that may affect measurement.

27. _____ occurs when there is a differential loss of respondents from comparison groups.

28. The problem of _____ occurs when subjects are allowed to decide whether they want to participate in a study.

29. The use of randomization controls potential threats to _____ validity.

30. A case study focusing on a single subject is known as a _____.

31. _____ involves the analysis of existing data.

32. If replicability cannot be achieved, the _____ of the observation is cast into doubt.

33. Most data are not merely stored but are subject to some form of _____.

34. The midpoint of a data series is the _____.

35. The likelihood of faulty findings in a test of significance increases as sample size _____.

36. In a research report, information about the authors of the report and their professional affiliations is usually found on the _____.

Multiple Choice

37. _____ research is undertaken for the sake of advancing scientific knowledge.
    a. Pure
    b. Applied
    c. Secondary
    d. Primary

38. The second stage of the research process is to
    a. develop a research design.
    b. review the findings.
    c. choose a data collection technique.
    d. identify a problem.

39. _____ is the process of turning a simple hypothesis into one that is testable.
    a. Theory building
    b. Variable development
    c. Operationalization
    d. Hypothesis testing

40. Given the following research design diagram, what does the "X" stand for?

    $$O_1 \quad X \quad O_2$$

    a. The pretest
    b. The post-test
    c. The experimental intervention
    d. None of the above

41. The problem of differential selection can be reduced through the use of
    a. statistical regression.
    b. random assignment.
    c. maturation.
    d. experimental mortality.

42. Which of the following factors is *not* a threat to external validity?
    a. Self-selection
    b. Multiple treatment interference
    c. Differential selection
    d. Reactive effects of testing

43. Which of the following is *not* a data-gathering strategy?
    a. Controlled experiment
    b. Participant observation
    c. Life history
    d. Secondary analysis

44. William Foote Whyte's study of Cornerville utilized the _____ strategy.
    a. participant observation
    b. life history
    c. survey
    d. case study

45. The data-gathering technique that does not produce new data is
    a. survey research.
    b. case study.
    c. participant observation.
    d. secondary analysis.

46. _____ means that when the same conditions exist, the same results can be expected to follow.
    a. Intersubjectivity
    b. Internal validity
    c. Replicability
    d. Randomization

47. Which of the following statistical techniques is an example of inferential statistics?
    a. The standard deviation
    b. A test of significance
    c. A degree of correlation
    d. The mean

48. Adding together all scores and dividing by the total number of observations yields the
    a. mean.
    b. median.
    c. mode.
    d. standard deviation.

49. A _____ correlation exists between sample size and the degree of confidence we can have in our results.
    a. curvilinear
    b. positive
    c. negative
    d. inverse

50. Techniques that produce measurable results that can be analyzed statistically are
    a. tests of significance.
    b. qualitative methods.
    c. intersubjectivity.
    d. quantitative methods.

51. Which of the following research methods produces quantitative data?
    a. Participant observation
    b. Life histories
    c. Case studies
    d. Controlled experiments

52. The principle of _____ means that research data are not shared outside the research environment.

    a. informed consent
    b. disclosure
    c. data confidentiality
    d. anonymity

53. Which of the following is *not* a critical ethical issue to researchers?

    a. Data confidentiality
    b. The protection of human subjects
    c. Disclosure of research methods
    d. Application of results to social policy

54. In a research report, the purpose of the _____ is to allow the author to make personal observations that may not be appropriate in the body of the report.

    a. abstract
    b. analysis
    c. introduction
    d. preface

Word Search Puzzle

```
E B S P V H X W K K C R S P M Z H H C A M C K L A
I U L P U I E R E S E A R C H R D I B T A R O W V
G G B F Z M S P K T Z F T F G O I K P D M K J B J
K C O N F I D E N T I A L I T Y C D K Q V Y T N Y
C Q E J A B E R X X G M X G E D F I V K F S L M C
A X A D Y V R Y L L J C N U R B V E R S T E H E N
F D R Q V A R I A B L E O Z R J O T X V X L L T Y
O P E R A T I O N A L I Z A T I O N H V D O N A M
R L K K I L X N K Y C L R Z D X O B J B X M S A X
K U D K J K X E Y Y S H Y P O T H E S I S O A N R
A F M Y N L B K B E F Y N F V M G Y Y A A Y O A W
B Z R A N D O M I Z A T I O N B J M Q Z Q T B L Q
P J N C B N T E X P E R I M E N T S M Q V Q C Y U
V I M O M L K R F D X T L E H F E Y E T A U S S A
Y M S I P C O N F O U N D I N G X L U Q L A U I L
M S D F F L K R T U O P U G E Y P Y P G I N R S I
Q A B C A S D B V Y R U Y T V N P H W R D T V X T
L C Y F G N H A P P L I E D Z X F E I Q I I E N A
P I N T E R S U B J E C T I V I T Y S W T T Y S T
N V E K J U L D F J M I G E W E D S G Z Y A B R I
S I I X X C A U L Z D E S C R I P T I V E T B E V
T A Q V N V K N D P I N F E R E N T I A L I L H E
O B Z D W T R E P L I C A B I L I T Y N G V H M B
V X B J L S T G F O O Q Q C Y G K B I V Y E H N C
M D N H U L Y S S K K P U E A G E E J T H E O R Y
```

Applied	Confounding	Confidentiality	Descriptive	Experiment
Hypothesis	Inferential	Intersubjectivity	Metaanalysis	Operationalization
Qualitative	Quantitative	Randomization	Replicability	Research
Survey	Theory	Validity	Variable	Verstehen

Crossword Puzzle

Across

2. _____ effects are rival explanations that threaten the validity of a research design.
4. The kind of subjective understanding achieved by criminologists who immerse themselves into the everyday world of the criminals they study.
6. The use of standardized, systematic procedures in the search for knowledge.
10. _____ validity is the ability to generalize research findings to other settings.
11. _____ validity is the certainty that the experimental interventions caused the changes observed in the study group.
14. A concept that can undergo measurable changes.
15. Research designed and carried out with practical applications in mind.
17. Research methods that produce measurable results.
18. _____ statistics describe or summarize relationships within data.
19. A series of interrelated propositions that attempt to describe, explain, predict, and control events.

Down

1. _____ statistics specify how likely findings are to be true for other populations.
3. The process by which concepts are made measurable.
5. The process by which individuals are assigned to study groups without selection biases.
7. Subjects who are not exposed to the experimental intervention (two words).
8. Research methods that produce subjective results.
9. A study of other studies.
12. An explanation that accounts for a set of facts and that can be tested by further investigation.
13. Valid observations made at one time can be made again at a later time if all other conditions are the same.
16. A type of research that gathers data through the use of questionnaires.

4 Classical and Neoclassical Thought

Learning Outcomes

After reading this chapter, students should be able to:

- Identify the major principles of the Classical School of criminological thought
- Explain the philosophical bases of classical thought
- Discuss the Enlightenment and describe its impact on criminological theorizing
- Identify modern-day practices that embody principles of the Classical School
- Explain the role of punishment in classical and neoclassical thought
- Discuss the policy implications of the Classical School
- Assess the shortcomings of the classical approach

Chapter Outline

Introduction
Major Principles of the Classical School
Forerunners of Classical Thought
    The Demonic Era
    Early Sources of the Criminal Law
    The Enlightenment
The Classical School
    Cesare Beccaria (1738–1794)
    Jeremy Bentham (1748–1832)
    Heritage of the Classical School
Neoclassical Criminology
    Rational Choice Theory
    The Seductions of Crime
    Situational Crime Control Policy
    Critique of Rational Choice Theory
Punishment and Neoclassical Thought
    Just Deserts
    Deterrence
    The Death Penalty
Policy Implications of the Classical School
A Critique of Classical Theories

Chapter Summary

This chapter introduces the Classical School of Criminology, which grew out of concepts and ideas developed by Enlightenment thinkers in the late seventeenth and early eighteenth centuries. It discusses the forerunners of classical thought, including the concepts of morality known as folkways and mores and the method of dividing crimes into the categories of *mala in se* (acts that are fundamentally wrong) and *mala prohibita* (acts that are wrong because they are prohibited). Early sources of the criminal law include the Code of Hammurabi, the Twelve Tables (the basis for early Roman law), English common law, and the Magna Carta, which was eventually expanded into the concept of due process.

The Enlightenment was a social movement that emphasized reason and rational thought. Key intellectual figures included Thomas Hobbes, John Locke, Montesquieu, Jean-Jacques Rousseau, and Thomas Paine. The Enlightenment conceptualized humans as rational beings possessing freedom of choice and led to the development of the Classical School of criminological thought, viewing crime and deviance as products of the exercise of free will. Cesare Beccaria, a key Enlightenment philosopher, published his *Essay on Crimes and Punishments* in 1764, setting forth his philosophy of punishment. Beccaria emphasized punishment based on the degree of injury caused, felt that the purpose of punishment should be deterrence (rather than retribution), and saw punishment as a tool to an end (crime prevention), rather than an end in itself. He emphasized the need for adjudication and punishment to be swift and for punishment, once decreed, to be certain. He also felt that punishment should only be severe enough to outweigh the personal benefits to be derived from crime. He opposed the use of torture and accepted the death penalty only for serious crimes against the state.

Jeremy Bentham, another founder of the Classical School, developed an approach known as utilitarianism or hedonistic calculus. Bentham believed that humans are rational and weigh the consequences of their behavior, considering pleasure versus pain. Therefore, he emphasized that to prevent crime, the pain of punishment must outweigh the pleasure derived from the crime. Like Beccaria, Bentham considered punishment to be a deterrent for those considering criminal activity.

The Classical School emphasized five basic principles, which are fundamental constituents of modern perspectives on crime and human behavior: rationality, hedonism, punishment, human rights, and due process.

By the start of the twentieth century, classical criminology was being replaced by positivism, which rejected the notion of free will and emphasized the concept of hard determinism: the belief that crime results from forces beyond the individual's control. However, by the 1970s, studies suggesting the failure of rehabilitation, combined with an increasing fear of crime, led to a resurgence of classical ideals known as neoclassical criminology.

Rational choice theory was developed out of the neoclassical school of criminology and is based on the belief that criminals make a conscious, rational, and at least partially informed choice to commit crime after weighing the costs and benefits of available alternatives. The two main varieties of choice theory are routine activities theory and situational choice theory. Routine activities theory suggests that crime is likely to occur when a motivated offender and suitable target come together in the absence of a capable guardian and focuses on how lifestyle can contribute to potential victimization. Situational choice theory revolves around the need for criminal opportunity and emphasizes the use of situational crime prevention strategies, such as defensible space, improved lighting, controlling alcohol sales at sporting events, etc. These theories have been criticized for overemphasizing individual choice, disregarding the role of social factors (poverty, poor home environment, inadequate socialization, etc.) on crime causation, and assuming that everyone is equally capable of making rational decisions. Their emphasis on situational crime prevention strategies may also result in displacement rather than true prevention.

Both classical and neoclassical thought emphasize punishment. However, the Classical School sees deterrence as the purpose of punishment while the neoclassical view also incorporates retribution: if an individual chooses to violate the law, he or she deserves punishment and must be punished. Just deserts is the sentencing model that refers to the notion that the offender deserves the punishment he or she receives at the hands of the law. Neoclassical thinkers distinguish between specific and general deterrence. For punishment to be an effective deterrent, it must be swift, certain, and severe enough to outweigh the rewards of the crime. However, these requirements are rarely met by the modern criminal justice system, which may explain the extremely high rates of recidivism in the United States.

The death penalty is probably the most controversial punishment. Research suggests it may not be an effective general deterrent and that it is applied inequitably. Many capital cases appear to be seriously flawed, resulting in the conviction of innocent individuals. There is also much concern over the disproportionate imposition of the death penalty on racial minorities. There is a large number of arguments both for and against the use of capital punishment in the United States.

There are a number of policy implications to come out of the Classical School, including the concepts of determinate sentencing, truth-in-sentencing laws, and incapacitation. Overall, the classical and neoclassical schools are more a philosophy of justice than a theory of crime causation. They do not explain how a choice for or against criminal activity is made nor do they take into account personal motivations. There is no scientific basis for the claims made by the Classical School and many neoclassical thinkers also emphasize philosophical ideals over scientific research.

Key Concepts

Capable guardian: One who effectively discourages crime.

Capital punishment: The legal imposition of a sentence of death upon a convicted offender. Also called *death penalty*.

Classical School: A criminological perspective of the late 1700s and early 1800s that had its roots in the Enlightenment and that held that humans are rational beings, that crime is the result of the exercise of free will, and that punishment can be effective in reducing the incidence of crime, as it negates the pleasure to be derived from crime commission.

Code of Hammurabi: An early set of laws established by the Babylonian King Hammurabi, who ruled the ancient city from 1792 to 1750 B.C.

Common law: Law originating from usage and custom rather than from written statutes. The term refers to nonstatutory customs, traditions, and precedents that help guide judicial decision making.

Dangerousness: The likelihood that a given individual will later harm society or others. Dangerousness is often measured in terms of recidivism, or the likelihood of new crime commission or rearrest for a new crime within a five-year period following arrest or release from confinement.

Determinate sentencing: A criminal punishment strategy that mandates a specified and fixed amount of time to be served for every offense category. Under the strategy, for example, all offenders convicted of the same degree of burglary would be sentenced to the same length of time behind bars. Also called *fixed sentencing*.

Deterrence: The prevention of crime. See also **general deterrence**; **specific deterrence**.

Displacement: A shift of criminal activity from one location to another.

Enlightenment: A social movement that arose during the eighteenth century and that built upon ideas such as empiricism, rationality, free will, humanism, and natural law. Also called *Age of Reason*.

Folkways: Time-honored customs. Although folkways carry the force of tradition, their violation is unlikely to threaten the survival of the group. See also **mores**.

General deterrence: A goal of criminal sentencing that seeks to prevent others from committing crimes similar to the one for which a particular offender is being sentenced.

Hard determinism: The belief that crime results from forces that are beyond the control of the individual.

Hedonistic calculus: The belief, first proposed by Jeremy Bentham, that behavior holds value to any individual undertaking it according to the amount of pleasure or pain that it can be expected to produce for that person. Also called *utilitarianism*.

Incapacitation: The use of imprisonment or other means to reduce the likelihood that an offender will be capable of committing future offenses.

Just deserts model: The notion that criminal offenders deserve the punishment they receive at the hands of the law and that punishments should be appropriate to the type and severity of crime committed.

Justice model: A contemporary model of imprisonment in which the principle of just deserts forms the underlying social philosophy.

Lifestyle theory: See **routine activities theory.**

Mala in se: Acts that are thought to be wrong in and of themselves.

Mala prohibita: Acts that are wrong only because they are prohibited.

Mores: Behavioral proscriptions covering potentially serious violations of a group's values. Examples include strictures against murder, rape, and robbery. See also **folkways**.

Natural law: The philosophical perspective that certain immutable laws are fundamental to human nature and can be readily ascertained through reason. Human-made laws, in contrast, are said to derive from human experience and history—both of which are subject to continual change.

Natural rights: The rights which, according to natural law theorists, individuals retain in the face of government action and interests.

Neoclassical criminology: A contemporary version of classical criminology that emphasizes deterrence and retribution, with reduced emphasis on rehabilitation.

Nothing-works doctrine: The belief popularized by Robert Martinson in the 1970s that correctional treatment programs have little success in rehabilitating offenders.

Panopticon: A prison designed by Jeremy Bentham that was to be a circular building with cells along the circumference, each clearly visible from a central location staffed by guards.

Positivism: The application of scientific techniques to the study of crime and criminals.

Rational choice theory: A perspective that holds that criminality is the result of conscious choice and that predicts that individuals choose to commit crime when the benefits outweigh the costs of disobeying the law.

Recidivism: The repetition of criminal behavior.

Recidivism rate: The percentage of convicted offenders who have been released from prison and who are later rearrested for a new crime, generally within five years following release. Also see **dangerousness**.

Retribution: The act of taking revenge upon a criminal perpetrator.

Routine activities theory (RAT): A brand of rational choice theory that suggests that lifestyles contribute significantly to both the volume and type of crime found in any society. Also called *lifestyle theory.*

Situational choice theory: A brand of rational choice theory that views criminal behavior "as a function of choices and decisions made within a context of situational constraints and opportunities."

Situational crime prevention: A social policy approach that looks to develop greater understanding of crime and more effective crime prevention strategies through concern with the physical, organizational, and social environments that make crime possible.

Social contract: The Enlightenment-era concept that human beings abandon their natural state of individual freedom to join together and form a society. In the process of forming a social contract, individuals surrender some freedoms to society as a whole, and government, once formed, is obligated to assume responsibilities toward its citizens and to provide for their protection and welfare.

Soft determinism: The belief that human behavior is the result of choices and decisions made within a context of situational constraints and opportunities.

Specific deterrence: A goal of criminal sentencing that seeks to prevent a particular offender from engaging in repeat criminality.

Target hardening: The reduction in criminal opportunity for a particular location, generally through the use of physical barriers, architectural design, and enhanced security measures.

Three-strikes legislation: Criminal statutes that mandate life imprisonment for criminals convicted of three violent felonies or serious drug offenses.

Trephination: A form of surgery typically involving bone, especially the skull. Early instances of cranial trephination have been taken as evidence for primitive beliefs in spirit possession.

Truth in sentencing: A close correspondence between the sentence imposed upon those sent to prison and the time actually served prior to prison release.

Twelve Tables: Early Roman laws written circa 450 B.C., which regulated family, religious, and economic life.

Utilitarianism: See **hedonistic calculus**.

Questions for Review

1. What were the central concepts that defined the Classical School of criminological thought?
2. Name the various preclassical thinkers identified in this chapter. What ideas did each contribute to Enlightenment philosophy? What form did those ideas take in classical criminological thought?
3. Identify the central figures in the Classical School, and explain the contributions of each.
4. What form does classical thought take today? What implications does such thought hold for crime control policy?
5. What role does punishment play in classical and neoclassical thinking about crime and crime prevention? According to this way of thinking, what kinds of punishment might work best to prevent crime?

6. What are the policy implications of the Classical School? What kinds of crime prevention and crime control programs might be based on classical principles?
7. What are the shortcomings of the Classical School? Of neoclassical thinking about crime and crime control?

Questions for Reflection

1. This book emphasizes a social problems versus social responsibility theme. Which perspective is most clearly supported by classical and neoclassical thought? Why?
2. Define *natural law*. Do you believe that natural law exists? If so, what types of behavior would be contravened by natural law? If not, why not?
3. What is meant by the idea of a social contract? How does the concept of social contract relate to natural law?
4. What were the central concepts that defined the Classical School of criminological thought? Which of those concepts are still alive? Where do you see evidence for the survival of those concepts?
5. Define *recidivism*. What is a recidivism rate? Why are recidivism rates so high today? What can be done to lower them?

Student Exercises

Activity #1

Your instructor will place you in groups and assign you to a public venue (a library, a grocery store, a video store, an office building, etc.). Your group is to inspect the location and answer the following questions:

1. What situational crime prevention techniques are in use in this location? What types of crime do they attempt to prevent? (For example, metal detectors help prevent the theft of library books.)
2. What additional techniques might be employed to reduce crime in this location?

Activity #2

Your instructor will place you into groups. Your group is to read the U.S. Constitution (including the Bill of Rights) and prepare a short report on how this document was influenced by the principles of the Classical School of Criminology, including specific examples.

Activity #3

Your instructor will provide you with a list of the UCR Part II offenses and ask you to classify each offense as either a *mala in se* or *mala prohibita* crime. You will then be placed into groups. Within each group, compare and contrast their classifications and determine where there is disagreement. Focus on the wide range of opinions present among a somewhat homogenous group (criminal justice majors at a university) and discuss possible reasons for these differing opinions.

Criminology Today on the Web

www.crimetheory.com/Archive/Beccaria/index.html

This site contains the text of Cesare Beccaria's *Essay On Crimes and Punishment*.

www.deathpenaltyinfo.org

This is the Web site for the Death Penalty Information Center, a nonprofit organization that provides the public with information on a variety of topics related to the issue of capital punishment.

www.yale.edu/lawweb/avalon/avalon.htm

This is the Web site for Yale University's Avalon Project. It includes the text of many legal and historical documents, including the Code of Hammurabi and the Magna Carta.

http://is.gseis.ucla.edu/impact/f96/Projects/dengberg

This site contains a virtual Panopticon for you to explore.

Student Study Guide Questions

True/False

_____ 1. The Classical School sees humans as fundamentally rational.

_____ 2. *Mala prohibita* acts are considered to be fundamentally wrong, regardless of the time or place in which they occur.

_____ 3. Thomas Hobbes had a very positive view of human nature and social life.

_____ 4. John Locke focused primarily on the responsibilities of individuals to the societies of which they are a part.

_____ 5. The Enlightenment contributed to the U.S. Constitution.

_____ 6. Beccaria emphasized punishing offenders based on an assessment of their criminal intent.

_____ 7. Beccaria was opposed to the death penalty under any circumstances.

_____ 8. Probation and victim restitution fall into Bentham's concept of compulsive punishment.

_____ 9. Soft determinism suggests that crime results from forces beyond the control of the individual.

_____ 10. Robert Martinson's research resulted in the development of the justice model.

_____ 11. According to Jack Katz, crime may be sensually compelling to the offender.

_____ 12. Situational crime prevention focuses on the context in which crime occurs.

_____ 13. According to modern neoclassical thinkers, if a person chooses to commit a crime, he or she deserves to be punished.

_____ 14. The deterrence rate is used to measure the success of a given approach to the problem of crime.

_____ 15. High recidivism rates suggest that criminal punishments do not effectively deter crime.

_____ 16. According to the Death Penalty Information Center, minorities are disproportionately represented on death row in the United States.

_____ 17. White defendants are rarely executed for the murder of a black victim.

_____ 18. Selective incapacitation removes groups of dangerous individuals from society by changing legislation or sentencing patterns.

Fill in the Blank

19. Of the terms used by Sumner, only _____ have been codified into formal strictures.

20. Criminal homicide is a _mala_ _____ crime.

21. The _____ is one of the first known bodies of law to survive to the present day.

22. Common law was declared the law of the land in England by King _____.

23. The concept of _____ suggests that certain immutable laws are fundamental to human nature and can be ascertained through reason.

24. According to Beccaria, oaths were _____ in a court of law.

25. The _____ principle of the Classical School emphasizes deterrence as the best justification for punishment.

26. _____ determinism is a belief that crime results from forces beyond an individual's control.

27. The statement that offenders deserve punishment because of the choices they make is typical of the _____ model.

28. _____ theory uses cost-benefit analysis.

29. Property identification falls into the _____ category of situational crime control.

30. Situational choice theory suggests that crime is a matter of both motivation and _____.

31. A(n) _____ decision relates to particular instances of criminal opportunity.

32. The _____ model of criminal sentencing involves the belief that criminal offenders deserve their punishment.

33. _____ is the repetition of criminal behavior by individuals who are already involved in crime.

34. _____ requires judges to assess and make public the actual time an offender is likely to serve once sentenced to prison.

35. The strategy of _____ uses imprisonment to reduce the likelihood that an offender will be capable of committing future offenses.

36. _____ uses changes in legislation or sentencing patterns to remove from society entire groups of individuals judged to be dangerous.

Multiple Choice

37. Which of the following statements would probably *not* be made by an adherent of the Classical School?
    a. I believe that punishment is necessary to deter criminals from committing more crimes.
    b. I believe that people have certain basic rights and that if the government infringes upon these rights, it should be dissolved.
    c. I believe that people's behavior is determined by pain and pleasure.
    d. I believe that forces beyond a person's control can affect his or her choice of criminal or noncriminal behavior.

38. _____ are time-honored customs that are preferred but which do not threaten the survival of the social group if they are violated.
    a. Mores
    b. Folkways
    c. Laws
    d. Crimes

39. Which of the following is *not* a *mala prohibita* crime?
    a. Gambling
    b. Premarital sexual behavior
    c. Drug use
    d. Theft

40. _____ was written around 450 B.C.
    a. The Code of Hammurabi
    b. The Common Law
    c. The Magna Carta
    d. The Twelve Tables

41. Which of the following works was written by Thomas Hobbes?
    a. *Essay Concerning Human Understanding*
    b. *The Spirit of Laws*
    c. *The Rights of Man*
    d. *Leviathan*

42. _____ punishment includes ordering an offender to make restitution.
    a. Pecuniary
    b. Compulsive
    c. Indelible
    d. Afflictive

43. The justice model was developed by
    a. Robert Martinson.
    b. David Fogel.
    c. Marcus Felson.
    d. Ronald V. Clarke.

44. According to routine activities theory, which of the following is *not* necessary for a crime to occur?
    a. The presence of a motivated offender
    b. The absence of a capable guardian
    c. The presence of a defensible victim
    d. The presence of a suitable target

45. The situational choice perspective was developed by
    a. Lawrence Cohen and Marcus Felson.
    b. Hal Pepinsky and Richard Quinney.
    c. Ronald Clarke and Derek Cornish.
    d. Walter DeKeseredy and Jock Young.

46. Rational choice theory emphasizes primarily
    a. pleasure and pain.
    b. emotionality.
    c. rationality and cognition.
    d. none of the above

47. Which of the following techniques falls into the situational crime control category of reducing the rewards?
    a. Formal surveillance
    b. Deflecting offenders
    c. Removing targets
    d. Facilitating compliance

48. Those who advocate _____ see the primary utility of punishment as revenge.
    a. deterrence
    b. retribution
    c. rehabilitation
    d. incapacitation

49. The Biblical injunction of "an eye for an eye" represents the concept of
    a. free will.
    b. just deserts.
    c. deterrence.
    d. rehabilitation.

50. According to modern-day advocates of general deterrence, which of the following is *not* required for punishment to be an effective impediment to crime?
    a. The punishment must be harsh.
    b. The punishment must be swift.
    c. The punishment must be severe.
    d. The punishment must be certain.

51. Recidivism rates in the United States reach levels of
    a. 10% to 20%.
    b. 40% to 50%.
    c. 60% to 70%.
    d. 80% to 90%.

52. In 2000, the governor of _____, George Ryan, suspended all executions in the state.
    a. Texas
    b. Illinois
    c. Georgia
    d. Maryland

53. Which of Lawrence Sherman's paradigms of justice most closely mirrors the principles of classical and neoclassical thought?
    a. Expressive economics
    b. Rational economics
    c. Expression
    d. Emotional intelligence

54. The use of imprisonment or other means to reduce the likelihood that an offender will be capable of committing future crimes is known as
    a. deterrence.
    b. retribution.
    c. rehabilitation.
    d. incapacitation.

Word Search Puzzle

```
X  T  D  G  W  H  C  L  A  X  J  O  F  D  K  P  Q  K  E  R  E  L  L  Q  N
S  U  L  G  C  N  T  Z  I  H  J  T  S  Z  T  G  I  S  M  O  Q  I  U  B  G
C  L  A  S  S  I  C  A  L  D  L  G  A  Y  R  E  T  R  I  B  U  T  I  O  N
J  B  H  D  I  S  P  L  A  C  E  M  E  N  T  C  U  Z  Q  W  V  N  E  V  L
B  P  L  Z  E  M  C  K  M  F  N  F  U  N  D  Q  K  C  Y  L  F  H  N  U  S
X  L  O  I  T  C  D  P  M  O  E  J  O  C  Q  Q  B  S  N  P  Y  K  L  F  G
F  G  A  Y  U  C  R  E  C  T  J  I  F  A  S  V  N  A  W  F  D  B  I  B  W
V  Z  I  A  O  B  W  I  K  L  T  X  C  C  C  O  T  U  W  H  C  D  G  E  R
L  O  V  U  Z  N  T  C  W  A  X  G  P  D  I  Y  E  E  M  Z  M  Q  H  M  R
O  B  S  G  X  P  T  N  T  A  U  K  W  T  X  X  S  Y  G  P  S  Y  T  X  E
P  I  L  L  O  N  S  I  M  A  N  P  A  B  V  Z  H  M  P  M  A  T  E  Q  P
P  C  G  N  Q  E  C  A  X  A  E  N  X  Z  M  K  X  M  G  K  W  N  N  R  O
J  S  A  Q  L  A  U  T  I  L  I  T  A  R  I  A  N  I  S  M  G  W  M  N  S
G  P  A  U  P  S  L  H  O  H  A  M  M  U  R  A  B  I  K  K  R  V  E  O  I
D  C  I  A  W  A  O  T  P  F  B  I  B  K  G  H  C  S  O  F  S  R  N  M  T
Y  I  C  F  R  H  F  E  Q  X  W  F  U  B  R  S  J  H  F  W  I  N  T  O  I
W  N  X  M  U  X  R  R  E  C  I  D  I  V  I  S  M  A  L  L  S  G  C  R  V
I  R  W  C  W  T  D  A  N  G  E  R  O  U  S  N  E  S  S  O  O  G  Z  E  I
R  K  D  E  T  E  R  M  I  N  I  S  M  G  N  I  G  D  X  V  O  O  L  S  S
U  H  R  Q  V  L  X  R  C  L  I  F  E  S  T  Y  L  E  O  X  G  O  W  J  M
U  W  K  S  K  B  D  S  U  J  U  A  D  E  T  E  R  R  E  N  C  E  S  L  A
K  W  F  U  V  Y  N  I  N  N  E  O  C  L  A  S  S  I  C  A  L  U  N  J  H
G  L  U  F  D  S  Y  U  P  J  A  T  R  L  G  F  B  O  G  V  Q  W  E  F  W
Y  L  F  E  A  Q  E  P  O  T  Q  F  I  F  B  H  W  J  Z  O  Z  U  E  T  H
D  E  J  Y  K  O  K  L  J  B  V  O  B  S  I  F  I  F  O  L  K  W  A  Y  S
```

Classical	Dangerousness	Determinism	Deterrence	Displacement
Enlightenment	Folkways	Hammurabi	Incapacitation	Lifestyle
Mores	Neoclassical	Panopticon	Positivism	Recidivism
Retribution	Trephination	Utilitarianism		

Crossword Puzzle

Across

2. The repetition of criminal behavior.
5. Time-honored customs that carry the force of tradition.
6. Acts that are wrong only because they are forbidden (two words).
8. The prevention of crime.
10. An eighteenth-century social movement that built upon the ideas of empiricism, rationality, free will, and natural law.
11. The notion that criminal offenders deserve the punishment they receive at the hands of the law (two words).
12. The type of deterrence that prevents a particular offender from recidivating.
14. Jeremy Bentham's circular prison design.
15. Taking revenge upon an offender.
16. The use of imprisonment to reduce an offender's ability to commit future crimes.
17. The application of scientific techniques to the study of crime and criminals.
18. Behavioral proscriptions covering potentially serious violations of a group's values.

Down

1. A form of surgery typically involving bone, especially the skull.
3. A shift of criminal activity from one location to another.
4. _____ crime prevention focuses on the environment that makes crime possible.
7. Early Roman laws that regulated family, religious, and economic life (two words).
8. The likelihood that a given individual will later harm society or others.
9. The _____ school suggests that humans are rational.
13. Acts that are thought to be wrong in and of themselves (three words).

5 Biological Roots of Criminal Behavior

Learning Outcomes

After reading this chapter, students should be able to:

- Identify the fundamental assumptions made by biological theories of crime causation
- Explain the relationship between human aggression and biological determinants
- Describe the research linking genetics and crime
- Explain the contributions of sociobiology to the study of criminality
- List some of the constitutional factors cited in this chapter as contributing to criminality
- Identify modern-day social policies that reflect the biological approach to crime causation
- Assess the shortcomings of biological theories of criminal behavior

Chapter Outline

Chapter Summary

This chapter introduces biological theories of human behavior, an area that generates a considerable amount of skepticism and controversy among criminologists. Many early biological theories fall into the category of criminal anthropology: the scientific study of the relationship between human physical characteristics and criminality. These include physiognomy, a theory with roots in ancient Greece, and phrenology, developed by Franz Joseph Gall and brought to the United States by Johann Gaspar Spurzheim. One of the best-known early positivists was Cesare Lombroso, who developed the theory of atavism, suggesting that most offenders are born criminals. He also identified other categories of offenders, including criminaloids, or occasional criminals, insane criminals, and criminals incited by passion. A number of later researchers evaluated atavism; Charles Goring found no support for the theory, while Earnest Hooton concluded that criminals were physiologically inferior. Hooton's work was extensively criticized by Steven Schafer.

Constitutional theories examine body types. One of the best known constitutional theories is somatotyping, a theory associated with Ernest Kretschmer and William H. Sheldon. Sheldon identified four main body types, linked them to personality, and concluded that the mesomorphic body type was most likely to be associated with criminality and delinquency.

Researchers have also linked criminal behavior to factors such as sugar or coffee consumption, food allergies, food additives, and vitamins, although the role of food and diet in producing criminal behavior has not been well established. Environmental pollution of lead, manganese, and other toxic metals also has been linked to violent crime. Prenatal exposure to substances such as tobacco smoke, alcohol, and marijuana have been found to be related to various behavioral factors, including delinquency. Various hormones, such as testosterone, serotonin, and cortisol, have been shown to be associated with aggression. Temperature also has been found to have an influence on both violent and property crime, although it is moderated by temporal factors such as the time of day and day of the week.

Research into criminal families, such as the Jukes and the Kallikaks, led to the development of eugenic criminology and the eugenics movement of the late 1920s and early 1930s; this has been largely discredited. Research into the XYY or "supermale" has also concluded that XYY males are not predictably aggressive. More recently, Dutch criminologists may have identified a specific gene with links to criminal behavior. The use of twins to study genetic influences has found support for a substantial influence of heredity on delinquent and criminal behavior. The Human Genome Project is helping to uncover more information about the role of genetics in criminality and is leading to a new view of genes as enabling rather than causing human action. Gender differences in criminal behavior have remained extremely regular over time, refuting claims of criminologists such as Freda Adler, who suggest that cultural changes producing increased opportunity for female criminality would lead to an increase in crimes by women.

Edward O. Wilson's paradigm of sociobiology involves systematic study of the biological basis of social behavior and emphasizes altruism and territoriality as determinants of behavior. Sociobiology has garnered considerable criticism as well as increased recognition.

A recent synthesis of biological and environmental factors was presented by James Q. Wilson and Richard Herrnstein in their book *Crime and Human Nature*. They identify a number of constitutional factors, such as age, gender, body type, intelligence, and personality, as contributing to crime. More recently, the concept of neuroplasticity has been advanced as a way to explain why some people experience significant personality changes while undergoing new experiences. Neuroplasticity suggests that the brain can alter its structure and function in response to new experiences; scientists now suggest that the brain is also malleable in response to internal stimuli (for example, thought).

The impact of biological theories on public policy has led to considerable controversy. Some fear issues such as racial prejudice or the resurgence of a new eugenics movement. In addition, contemporary criminologists have provided focused critiques of biological perspectives on crime, including methodological and other concerns. It does appear that various biological factors are correlated with various measures of criminal behavior, although the influence of social factors has overshadowed the relationship.

Key Concepts

Atavism: A concept used by Cesare Lombroso to suggest that criminals are physiological throwbacks to earlier stages of human evolution. The term is derived from the Latin term *atavus*, which means "ancestor."

Behavioral genetics: The study of genetic and environmental contributions to individual variations in human behavior.

Biological theory: A theory that maintains that the basic determinants of human behavior, including criminality, are constitutionally or physiologically based and often inherited.

Born criminal: An individual who is born with a genetic predilection toward criminality.

Constitutional theory: A theory that explains criminality by reference to offenders' body types, inheritance, genetics, or external observable physical characteristics.

Criminal anthropology: The scientific study of the relationship between human physical characteristics and criminality.

Criminaloids: A term used by Cesare Lombroso to describe occasional criminals who were pulled into criminality primarily by environmental influences.

Cycloid: A term developed by Ernst Kretschmer to describe a particular relationship between body build and personality type. The cycloid personality, which was associated with a heavyset, soft type of body, was said to vacillate between normality and abnormality.

Displastic: A mixed group of offenders described by constitutional theorist Ernst Kretschmer as highly emotional and often unable to control themselves. They were thought to commit mostly sexual offenses and other crimes of passion. The term is largely of historical interest.

Ectomorph: A body type originally described as thin and fragile, with long, slender, poorly muscled extremities and delicate bones.

Endomorph: A body type originally described as soft and round or overweight.

Eugenic criminology: A perspective that holds that the root causes of criminality are passed from generation to generation in the form of "bad genes."

Eugenics: The study of hereditary improvement by genetic control.

Genetic determinism: The belief that genes are the major determining factor in human behavior.

Heritability: A statistical construct that estimates the amount of variation in a population that is attributable to genetic factors.

Hypoglycemia: A medical condition characterized by low blood sugar.

Juke family: A well-known "criminal family" studied by Richard L. Dugdale.

Kallikak family: A well-known "criminal family" studied by Henry H. Goddard.

Masculinity hypothesis: (1) A belief (from the late 1800s) that criminal women typically exhibited masculine features and mannerisms. (2) In the late 1900s, the belief that, over time, men and women will commit crimes that are increasingly similar in nature, seriousness, and frequency. Increasing similarity in crime commission is predicted to result from changes in the social status of women (for example, better economic position, gender role convergence, socialization practices that are increasingly similar for both males and females, and so on).

Mesomorph: A body type described as athletic and muscular.

Monozyotic (MZ) twins: Twins that develop from the same egg and that carry virtually the same genetic material.

Paradigm: An example, a model, or a theory.

Phrenology: The study of the shape of the head to determine anatomical correlates of human behavior.

Schizoid: A person characterized by schizoid personality disorder. Such disordered personalities appear to be aloof, withdrawn, unresponsive, humorless, dull, and solitary to an abnormal degree.

Sociobiology: "The systematic study of the biological basis of all social behavior."

Somatotyping: The classification of human beings into types according to body build and other physical characteristics.

Supermale: A male individual displaying the XYY chromosome structure.

Testosterone: The primary male sex hormone. Produced in the testes, its function is to control secondary sex characteristics and sexual drive.

Questions for Review

1. What are the central assumptions of biological theories of crime? How do such theories differ from other perspectives that attempt to explain the same phenomena?
2. What biological factors does this chapter suggest might substantially influence human aggression?
3. What have research studies in the field of genetics had to say about possible causes of crime?
4. What is sociobiology? How do sociobiologists explain criminality?
5. What are some of the constitutional factors that this chapter identifies as linked to criminality?
6. What are the social policy implications of biological theories of crime? What U.S. Supreme Court case, discussed in this chapter, might presage a type of policy based on such theories?
7. Why have biological approaches to crime causation encountered stiff criticism? Do you agree or disagree with those who are critical of such perspectives? Why?

Questions for Reflection

1. This book emphasizes a social problems versus social responsibility theme. Which perspective is best supported by biological theories of crime causation? Why?
2. What does the author of this book mean when he writes, "Open inquiry . . . requires objective consideration of all points of view and an unbiased examination of each for their ability to shed light on the subject under study"? Do you agree or disagree with this assertion? Why?

Student Exercises

Activity #1

Watch several episodes of a reality-based television show such as *Cops*. Observe the suspects in each crime/event and record as much information as possible about their physical characteristics. Do you notice any common physical characteristics among the suspects? Does there appear to be a "criminal type"?

In addition, watch several episodes of a nonreality-based show and record information about the physical characteristics of the actors playing the criminals. Do fictional television shows cast actors of a certain physical type to play offenders? What characteristics (if any) are common to fictional criminals?

Activity #2

Review the elements that C. Ray Jeffrey states should be included in a comprehensive biologically based program of crime prevention and control. Discuss the ethical implications of these components.

Activity #3

In your university library, obtain information on the Youth Violence Initiative, a program proposed during the Bush administration in the early 1990s. Do you think that this program should have been canceled by President Clinton? Why or why not?

Criminology Today on the Web

www3.niu.edu/acad/psych/Millis/History/2004/phrenology.htm

This Web site houses an article about phrenology and the ideas behind it.

www.crimetheory.com/Archive/BvB/index.html

This Web site includes information on the U.S. Supreme Court's 1927 ruling in the case of *Buck* v. *Bell*.

www.ornl.gov/sci/techresources/Human_Genome/home.shtml

This is the home page of the Human Genome Project.

www.crime-times.org

This is the Web site of *Crime Times*, a national newsletter reporting on research conducted in the area of biological causes of crime.

Student Study Guide Questions

True/False

_____ 1. Biological theories consider the brain to be the locus of personality.

_____ 2. Charles Darwin wrote the book *On Aggression*.

_____ 3. Criminal anthropology is the scientific study of the relationship between human physical characteristics and criminality.

_____ 4. Positivism emphasizes observation and measurement.

_____ 5. Criminaloids do not exhibit atavism.

_____ 6. Earnest Hooton favored the development of rehabilitation programs.

_____ 7. Hooton took into consideration the fact that some members of his noncriminal control group may have been criminals who had not been caught and processed by the criminal justice system.

_____ 8. Ernst Kretschmer's cycloid personality was associated with an athletic and muscular body.

_____ 9. The criminal courts do not agree that excess sugar consumption may be linked to crime.

_____ 10. Food additives have been found to produce criminal violence.

_____ 11. Increased levels of testosterone may be linked to increased aggressiveness in men.

_____ 12. PMS as a defense has been accepted by the courts.

_____ 13. Weather has no significant influence on human behavior.

_____ 14. Research does not support the notion of a link between barometric pressure and crime.

_____ 15. Lawrence E. Hannell was acquitted of murder because he was found to be a supermale.

_____ 16. The proportion of homicides committed by men versus women has remained fairly constant for the last 40 years.

_____ 17. Wilson and Herrnstein said that individuals commit more crimes as they get older.

_____ 18. It is possible for researchers conducting twin studies to make errors when classifying a pair of twins as monozygotic or dizygotic.

Fill in the Blank

19. Biological theories of crime causation assume that the basic determinants of behavior are _____ based.

20. Biological theories would suggest that _____ differences in criminality may be due in part to biological differences between the sexes.

21. According to Gall, the shape of the _____ is indicative of the personality.

22. _____ conducted a study of Lombroso's theory and concluded that criminals show an overall physiological inferiority to the general population.

23. _____ theories focus on an offender's body type.

24. Early studies of chemical imbalances linked _____ to murder.

25. Research suggests that _____ brain levels of serotonin might reduce aggression.

26. According to research, specific shades of the color _____ could have a calming effect on people experiencing feelings of anger and agitation.

27. Men whose brains lack sufficient amounts of _____ may feel frustration more acutely and respond to frustrating circumstances more aggressively.

28. Research has found a _____ correlation between temperature and violent crime.

29. Richard Dugdale studied the _____ family.

30. _____ criminology focuses on the idea that the root causes of criminality are passed from one generation to the next in the form of "bad genes."

31. The eugenics movement policies were endorsed by the U.S. Supreme Court in the case of _____.

32. _____ was the first Western scientist to systematically study heredity and its possible influence on human behavior.

33. Identical twins are known as _____ twins.

34. The concept of _____ in sociobiology is used to explain conflict between humans.

35. According to Wilson and Herrnstein, criminality is consistently associated with _____ intelligence.

36. According to _____, a comprehensive biologically based crime prevention program would include prenatal and postnatal care for pregnant women and their infants.

Multiple Choice

37. Which of the following is *not* one of the fundamental assumptions of biological theories of crime causation?
    a. The brain is the organ of behavior.
    b. The basic determinants of criminal behavior are, to a considerable degree, the product of individual choice.
    c. A tendency to commit crime may be inherited.
    d. They are all fundamental assumptions of biological theories.

38. The early biological theory that predicted personality characteristics from human facial features was known as

   a. atavism.
   b. physiognomy.
   c. somatotyping.
   d. phrenology.

39. The early biological theory that studied the shape of the head to predict criminality was known as

   a. atavism.
   b. physiognomy.
   c. somatotyping.
   d. phrenology.

40. _____ is a concept used by Cesare Lombroso to suggest that criminality is the result of primitive urges that survived the evolutionary process.

   a. Ectomorph
   b. Atavism
   c. Schizoid
   d. Criminaloid

41. An atavistic individual has an underdeveloped _____.

   a. brain.
   b. personality.
   c. emotional state.
   d. physique.

42. According to Cesare Lombroso's categorization of offenders, occasional criminals were known as

   a. criminaloids.
   b. atavists.
   c. insane.
   d. criminals incited by passion.

43. _____ reported finding physiological features characteristic of specific criminal types in individual states.

   a. Cesare Lombroso
   b. Earnest Hooton
   c. Charles Goring
   d. William Sheldon

44. Which of the following was *not* one of Ernst Kretschmer's mental categories?

   a. Schizoids
   b. Criminaloids
   c. Cycloids
   d. Displastics

45. Which of the following was *not* one of William Sheldon's basic body types?

    a. Ectomorphs
    b. Endomorphs
    c. Mesomorphs
    d. Cyclothmorphs

46. Which of Sheldon's body types is most likely to be relaxed and sociable?

    a. An ectomorph
    b. An endomorph
    c. A mesomorph
    d. A cyclothmorph

47. Which of the following foods has *not* been implicated in the production of criminal violence?

    a. Coffee
    b. MSG
    c. Processed foods
    d. All of the above may possibly trigger antisocial behavior.

48. The relationship between testosterone and aggressive behavior in young males appears to be moderated by

    a. age.
    b. the social environment.
    c. genetics.
    d. none of the above

49. The agitation and irritability sometimes associated with premenstrual syndrome may be explained by a decrease in _____ levels in the female brain just before menstruation.

    a. serotonin
    b. dopamine
    c. testosterone
    d. cortisol

50. According to Cohn and Rotton, the relationship between temperature and assaults is strongest during the _____ hours.

    a. evening
    b. morning
    c. afternoon
    d. midday

51. The studies of the Jukes and Kallikak families emphasized _____ as the primary source of criminality.

    a. environment
    b. ecology
    c. genetics
    d. psychology

52. The purpose of the Human Genome Project is to determine the complete sequence of
    a. DNA.
    b. RNA.
    c. XYY.
    d. MAOA.

53. Sociobiology was introduced by
    a. Freda Adler.
    b. Arnold L. Lieber.
    c. James Q. Wilson.
    d. Edward O. Wilson.

54. The _____ myth holds that everyone has an individual soul-like quality that can make choices independent of any biological predispositions.
    a. Blank Slate
    b. Noble Savage
    c. Ghost in the Machine
    d. Scientific Method

Word Search Puzzle

```
E U G E N I C S D Y I L P F S B L K O D Y K N T C
H I H T W T J R U F O G C S N N E C G R Q E R R I
L M P O W T M B A K W S W N O E C Y R I W H H V C
M Q S U P E R M A L E J R C Y A L C J E D X Z M R
N L Z D R J K A G B P Z E V Q G N L N N X E U L I
T D M B F H U A V Q K X Y H P B M O V D W A A F M
G I I G J S X F E J Z Z K Q R E L I K O T O T Y I
N B Q I N R E L R K E B C S O V M D Q M W S J H N
O F M P D I S P L A S T I C J D O B V O V O N L A
S L Z K S U B X P H R E N O L O G Y H R R C Y B L
E N O F P K I P T V K E U A C O Q G R P I I T T O
E C T O M O R P H Y U X X P D H V C Y H G O F N I
G K G E Z A L Q V E M E S O M O R P H D J B S R D
Y I T X M C V D R E I G H B U M N D T L I I O Y S
N S Z O I H A R S G L X F X W E M T Z J Z O K T Z
Y B H E R I T A B I L I T Y S E Z X S U U L R T M
M H Y P O G L Y C E M I A O Z E A D K K F O P A L
T V F O L F K N Y Q M L D O Y T C Y S E V G X S F
O P E T N G N W V W S L G P S Z E F C A P Y X S G
E M F Q T E S T O S T E R O N E P A R A D I G M E
F I Z E S C H I Z O I D R R H H A I S J B T B N K
P E D B J P V H U Z H W K T D B J S G Q H U S G U
A B V G Y X G V A X V R B G M O N O Z Y G O T I C
S O M A T O T Y P I N G R A T A V I S M R X E Q O
W D R Q Y L P E T V S W O B J C K A L L I K A K G
```

Atavism	Criminaloids	Cycloid	Displastic	Ectomorph	Endomorph
Eugenics	Heritability	Hypoglycemia	Juke	Kallikak	Mesomorph
Monozygotic	Paradigm	Phrenology	Schizoid	Sociobiology	Somatotyping
Supermale	Testosterone				

Crossword Puzzle

Across

1. Ernst Kretschmer's term describing a mixed group of offenders who are often unable to control themselves.
4. The amount of variation in a population attributable to genetic factors.
6. The study of hereditary improvement by genetic control.
7. Cesare Lombroso's term describing occasional criminals pulled into criminality by environmental influences.
9. Twins that develop from the same egg.
11. An individual displaying the XYY chromosome structure.
13. A body type that is athletic and muscular.
14. A body type that is thin and fragile.
15. The systematic study of the biological basis of all social behavior.
16. Classifying humans according to body build.

Down

2. Cesare Lombroso's concept that criminals are physiological throwbacks to earlier stages of human evolution.
3. The primary male sex hormone.
4. A condition characterized by low blood sugar.
5. A body type that is soft and round.
8. The study of the shape of the head to determine anatomical correlates of human behavior.
10. Ernst Kretschmer's term describing a personality associated with a heavyset, soft type of body.
12. An example, model, or theory.

6 Psychological and Psychiatric Foundations of Criminal Behavior

Learning Outcomes

After reading this chapter, students should be able to:

- Identify the major principles of psychological perspectives as they relate to criminal behavior
- List and describe some early psychological and psychiatric theories that purported to explain criminality
- Understand how criminality can be seen as a form of maladaptive behavior
- Understand how criminality can be seen as a form of adaptive behavior
- Describe the modeling theory of aggression and explain how aggressive patterns of behavior can be activated
- Describe behavior theory and explain the role of rewards and punishments in shaping behavior
- Explain attachment theory and describe the three forms of attachment
- Define *self-control* and describe how a lack of self-control can lead to crime
- Illustrate the legal concept of insanity and delineate the various legal standards for determining insanity
- Identify the types of crime control policies that might be based on psychological understandings of criminality
- Delineate the assumptions underlying the practice of criminal psychological profiling

Chapter Outline

Chapter Summary

This chapter introduces psychological and psychiatric theories of human behavior. Most early psychological theories emphasized either behavioral conditioning or personality disturbances and diseases of the mind. The concept of the psychopath or sociopath was developed by Hervey Cleckley. Currently, these terms have fallen out of favor and have been replaced by the concept of antisocial personality. Individuals with the characteristics of an antisocial personality are likely to become criminals at some point. Another theory emphasizing personality characteristics was developed by Hans Eysenck. Eysenck described three personality dimensions (psychoticism, extroversion, and neuroticism), each with links to criminality. He stated that personality traits were dependent on the autonomic nervous system; those whose nervous systems require stimulation are more likely to become offenders.

Psychiatric criminology envisions a complex set of motives and drives operating from hidden recesses deep within the personality to determine behavior. Sigmund Freud's psychoanalytic theory suggests that criminal behavior is maladaptive, the result of inadequacies inherent in the offender's personality. Psychoanalysis suggests that one possible cause of crime may be a poorly developed superego, which leaves the individual operating without a moral guide. Neurosis, a minor form of mental illness, may also lead to crime. In addition, more serious mental illness, such as psychosis, may result in criminal behavior, including violent crime. Freud's frustration–aggression link was more fully developed by researchers such as J. Dollard, who suggested that everyone suffers frustration and thus aggression is a natural part of life; it may be manifested in socially acceptable or unacceptable ways. Other theorists suggest that crime fulfills some purpose, such as the need to be punished or the need to reduce stress.

Modeling theory, as developed by Albert Bandura, is a form of social learning theory that suggests that people learn to act by observing others; observation of aggressive behavior teaches one how to behave aggressively. Behavior theory, developed by researchers such as B.F. Skinner, involves the use of rewards and punishments to control a person's responses, or operant behavior. Attachment theory suggests that the lack of a secure attachment between a child and his or her primary caregiver may lead to delinquent and criminal behavior later in life. Michael Gottfredson and Travis Hirschi developed a general theory of crime based on the concept that low self-control accounts for all types of crime.

Insanity is a legal rather than a clinical concept and is based on the claim of mental illness. Insanity is a defense to criminal prosecution and the burden of proof is on the defendant; a person is presumed sane at the start of a criminal trial. The 1984 federal Insanity

Defense Reform Act (IDRA) created the verdict of not guilty by reason of insanity (NGRI), ensured that a federal defendant found NGRI will be hospitalized rather than released, and included a provision permitting mentally ill persons to be held for trial in the hopes that they will recover sufficiently to permit the trial to proceed. Several tests for insanity are used in the United States. The *M'Naughten* rule holds that people cannot be held criminally responsible for their actions if at the time of the crime they either did not know what they were doing or did not know that what they were doing was wrong. The irresistible-impulse test, which can be used alone or in conjunction with *M'Naughten*, holds that people are not guilty of criminal offenses if by virtue of their mental state or psychological condition, they were unable to resist committing the criminal act. Other tests include the *Durham* rule, the substantial-capacity test, and the *Brawner* rule. Some states permit verdicts of guilty but mentally ill (GBMI), which allows the defendant to be held responsible for a crime despite the presence of some degree of mental incompetence.

The use of psychological theories to predict or assess dangerousness has contributed to social policy. The concept of selective incapacitation is based on the notion of career criminals and relies on prediction of future criminality to determine sentencing policy. Correctional psychology is concerned with the diagnosis and classification of offenders, the treatment of correctional populations, and the rehabilitation of offenders. Criminal psychological profiling is used to help police better understand people wanted for serious crimes.

Key Concepts

Alloplastic adaptation: A form of adjustment that results from changes in the environment surrounding an individual.

Antisocial (asocial) personality: A term used to describe individuals who are basically unsocialized and whose behavior pattern brings them repeatedly into conflict with society.

Antisocial personality disorder: A psychological condition exhibited by individuals who are basically unsocialized and whose behavior pattern brings them repeatedly into conflict with society.

Attachment theory: A social-psychological perspective on delinquent and criminal behavior that holds that the successful development of secure attachment between a child and his or her primary caregiver provides the basic foundation for all future psychological development.

Autoplastic adaptation: A form of adjustment that results from changes within an individual.

Behavior theory: A psychological perspective that posits that individual behavior that is rewarded will increase in frequency, while that which is punished will decrease.

***Brawner* rule:**   A somewhat vague rule for determining insanity that was created in the 1972 federal court case of *U.S.* v. *Brawner* (471 F.2d 969), since superseded by statute, and asks the jury to decide whether the defendant could be *justly* held responsible for the criminal act with which he or she stands charged, in the face of any claims of insanity or mental incapacity.

Conditioning: A psychological principle that holds that the frequency of any behavior can be increased or decreased through reward, punishment, or association with other stimuli.

Correctional psychology: The branch of forensic psychology concerned with the diagnosis and classification of offenders, the treatment of correctional populations, and the rehabilitation of inmates and other law violators.

Criminal psychology: See **forensic psychology**.

***Durham* rule:**   A standard for judging legal insanity that holds that an accused is not criminally responsible if his or her unlawful act was the product of mental disease or mental defect.

Ego: The reality-testing part of the personality. Also called the *reality principle*. More formally, the personality component that is conscious, most immediately controls behavior, and is most in touch with external reality.

Electroencephalogram (EEG):   The electrical measurement of brain wave activity.

Forensic psychiatry: A branch of psychiatry having to do with the study of crime and criminality.

Forensic psychology: The application of the science and profession of psychology to questions and issues relating to law and the legal system.

Guilty but mentally ill (GBMI):   A finding that offenders are guilty of the criminal offense with which they are charged, but because of their prevailing mental condition, they are generally sent to psychiatric hospitals for treatment rather than to prison. Once they have been declared cured, however, such offenders can be transferred to correctional facilities to serve out their sentences.

Id: The aspect of the personality from which drives, wishes, urges, and desires emanate. More formally, the division of the psyche associated with instinctual impulses and demands for immediate satisfaction of primitive needs.

Insanity

Insanity (legal):   A legally established inability to understand right from wrong or to conform one's behavior to the requirements of the law.

Insanity (psychological):   Persistent mental disorder or derangement.

Irresistible-impulse test: A standard for judging legal insanity that holds that a defendant is not guilty of a criminal offense if the person, by virtue of his or her mental state or psychological condition, was not able to resist committing the crime.

***M'Naughten* rule:**   A standard for judging legal insanity that requires that offenders not know what they were doing, or if they did, that they not know it was wrong.

Modeling theory: A form of social learning theory that asserts that people learn how to act by observing others.

Neurosis: A functional disorder of the mind or of the emotions involving anxiety, phobia, or other abnormal behavior.

Operant behavior: Behavior that affects the environment in such a way as to produce responses or further behavioral cues.

Paranoid schizophrenic: A schizophrenic individual who suffers from delusions and hallucinations.

Psychiatric criminology: Theories that are derived from the medical sciences, including neurology, and that, like other psychological theories, focus on the individual as the unit of analysis. Psychiatric theories form the basis of psychiatric criminology. See also **forensic psychiatry.**

Psychoanalysis: The theory of human psychology founded by Sigmund Freud on the concepts of the unconscious, resistance, repression, sexuality, and the Oedipus complex.

Psychological profiling: The attempt to categorize, understand, and predict the behavior of certain types of offenders based on behavioral clues they provide.

Psychological theory: A theory derived from the behavioral sciences that focuses on the individual as the unit of analysis. Psychological theories place the locus of crime causation within the personality of the individual offender.

Psychopath: An individual with a personality disorder, especially one manifested in aggressively antisocial behavior, and who is lacking in empathy. Also called *sociopath*.

Psychopathy: A personality disorder characterized by antisocial behavior and lack of affect.

Psychosis: A form of mental illness in which sufferers are said to be out of touch with reality.

Psychotherapy: A form of psychiatric treatment based on psychoanalytical principles and techniques.

Punishment: An undesirable behavioral consequence likely to decrease the frequency of occurrence of that behavior.

Reward: A desirable behavioral consequence likely to increase the frequency of occurrence of that behavior.

Schizophrenic: A mentally ill individual who is out of touch with reality and who suffers from disjointed thinking.

Selective incapacitation: A social policy that seeks to protect society by incarcerating the individuals deemed to be the most dangerous.

Self-control: A person's ability to alter his or her own states and responses.

Sociopath: See **psychopath**.

Sublimation: The psychological process whereby one aspect of consciousness comes to be symbolically substituted for another.

Substantial-capacity test: A standard for judging legal insanity that requires that a person lack the mental capacity needed to understand the wrongfulness of his or her act or to conform his or her behavior to the requirements of the law.

Superego: The moral aspect of the personality; much like the conscience. More formally, the division of the psyche that develops by the incorporation of the perceived moral standards of the community, is mainly unconscious, and includes the conscience.

Thanatos: A death wish.

Questions for Review

1. What are the major principles of psychological perspectives as they relate to criminal behavior?
2. Which of the early psychological and psychiatric theories that were offered explain criminality?
3. From a psychological perspective, how can criminal behavior be seen as a type of maladaptive behavior?
4. How can crime commission be a form of adaptive behavior?
5. How does modeling theory explain the occurrence of criminality? How might aggressive patterns of behavior, once acquired, be activated?
6. What are the principles underlying behavior theory? How can rewards and punishments shape behavior?

7. What are the principles of attachment theory? What are the three forms of attachment discussed in this chapter?
8. How can a lack of self-control lead to crime? What can be done to enhance self-control?
9. What is insanity under the criminal law? What are the various legal standards for determining insanity?
10. What types of crime control policies might be based on psychological understandings of criminality?
11. What are the main assumptions underlying the practice of criminal psychological profiling?

Questions for Reflection

1. This book emphasizes a social problems versus social responsibility theme. Which perspective is best supported by psychological theories of crime causation? Why?
2. How do psychological theories of criminal behavior differ from the other types of theories presented in this book? How do the various psychological and psychiatric approaches presented in this chapter differ from one another?
3. How would the perspectives discussed in this chapter suggest that offenders might be prevented from committing additional offenses? How might they be rehabilitated?
4. How can crime be a form of adaptation to one's environment? Why would an individual choose such a form of adaptation over others that might be available?
5. Which of the various standards for judging legal insanity discussed in this chapter do you find the most useful? Why?

Student Exercises

Activity #1

Your instructor will assign you a state. Go to the Web site of the Cornell University Law School's Legal Information Institute at www.law.cornell.edu, locate the statutes for this state, and find the definition of the insanity defense. Answer the following questions:

1. What test or tests are used to determine legal insanity?
2. Is the defendant presumed to be sane until proven otherwise?
3. Does the burden of proof for the defense of insanity lie with the defense or the prosecution?
4. If legal insanity is proved, what verdict is used, NGRI or GBI?

Activity #2

Your instructor will place you in groups. Within your group, discuss different ways that you were taught right from wrong as a child. Using behavior theory, classify these techniques as positive rewards, negative rewards, positive punishments, or negative punishments. Which of the four types of rewards and punishments seemed to be most effective?

Criminology Today on the Web

www.healthyminds.org/insanitydefense.cfm

This Web site provides information on the insanity defense from the American Psychiatric Association.

www.forensic-psych.com/articles/artRebirth.html

This Web site contains an article on forensic psychiatry and the insanity defense.

www.mentalhealth.com/dis/p20-pe04.html http://health. discovery.com/encyclopedias/illnesses.html?article=2797

These two sites provide information on antisocial personality disorder.

http://faculty.ncwc.edu/toconnor/428/428lect01.htm

This Web site makes available an article on the history of profiling.

http://mentalhelp.net

This site provides information on mental health, disorders, and treatments.

Student Study Guide Questions

True/False

_____ 1. Forensic psychologists generally hold Ph.D. degrees.

_____ 2. According to psychological theories, crimes result from normal and appropriate mental processes within the personality.

_____ 3. Poor intelligence is a characteristic of the psychopathic personality.

_____ 4. Individuals suffering from antisocial personality disorder generally show a persistent disregard for social norms and rules.

_____ 5. Females with antisocial personality disorder exhibit different characteristics than their male counterparts.

_____ 6. According to Eysenck, introverts rarely become criminal offenders.

_____ 7. The superego is a moral guide to right and wrong.

_____ 8. According to Alfredo Niceforo, the superior ego developed as a consequence of socialization.

_____ 9. A neurosis is a serious form of mental illness.

_____ 10. Frustration-aggression theory argues that aggression is a natural consequence of living.

_____ 11. When crime leads to stress reduction as a result of internal changes in beliefs and value systems, it is referred to as alloplastic adaptation.

_____ 12. According to Gabriel Tarde, individuals imitate the behavior of those they are in close contact with.

_____ 13. According to Bandura, aggressive behavior can be learned through watching television.

_____ 14. People who devalue aggression do not engage in it.

_____ 15. Attachment theory suggests that anxious-avoidant attachment results in feelings of uncertainty.

_____ 16. Gottfredson and Hirschi suggest that self-control develops in adulthood.

_____ 17. The substantial capacity test is used in every state in the country.

_____ 18. In their book *The Psychology of Criminal Conduct*, D. A. Andrews and James Bonta are attempting to develop a new behavioral theory.

Fill in the Blank

19. _____ psychology applies psychology to questions and issues relating to law and the legal system.

20. A psychopath is also known as a(n) _____.

21. _____ causes of antisocial personality disorder are based on physiological features.

22. The inability to identify with one's parents during childhood and adolescence is a possible _____ cause of antisocial personality disorder.

23. Eysenck attributes up to _____ of all behavioral variance to a strong genetic basis.

24. _____ criminology envisions a complex set of drives and motives operating from hidden recesses deep within the personality to determine behavior.

25. Desires, wishes, and urges emanate from the _____, according to Freud.

26. If the superego does not function properly, the mind falls back on the reality-testing ability of the _____.

27. A(n) _____ psychosis has no known physical cause.

28. According to Gabriel Tarde, the basis of any society is physical cause._____

29. _____ theory is the "stimulus–response approach" to human patterns of being.

30. John Bowlby developed the _____ theory of crime and delinquency.

31. _____ refers to a person's ability to alter his or her own states and responses.

32. Pratt and Cullen suggest that _____ self-control is one of the strongest known correlates of crime.

33. After attempting to assassinate then-President Ronald Reagan, _____ was acquitted of the charges against him on the grounds of insanity.

34. According to the Insanity Defense Reform Act, the burden of proving insanity is placed on the _____. According to the Insanity Defense Reform Act, the burden of proving insanity is placed on the _____.

35. According to the *Durham* rule, _____ is a condition that is considered capable of improving or deteriorating.

36. The _____ combines elements of the *M'Naughten* rule and the irresistible-impulse test.

Multiple Choice

37. Which of the following is *not* a fundamental assumption of most psychological theories of crime causation?
    a. The major motivational element within a person is personality.
    b. Defective mental processes may have a variety of causes.
    c. Crimes result from individual choice.
    d. Normality is generally defined by social consensus.

38. The concept of a psychopathic personality was developed by
    a. Hans Eysenck.
    b. Ivan Pavlov.
    c. Hervey Cleckley.
    d. Albert Bandura.

39. Which of the following is *not* one of the characteristics of the psychopathic personality described by Cleckley?
    a. Superficial charm
    b. Chronic lying
    c. Unreliability
    d. Low intelligence

40. Which of the following was *not* one of the three personality dimensions described by Hans Eysneck in his study of personality characteristics and crime?
    a. Extroversion
    b. Schizophrenism
    c. Psychoticism
    d. Neuroticism

41. According to Freud's psychoanalytic theory, the id conforms to the
    a. reality principle.
    b. pleasure principle.
    c. morality and conscience.
    d. unconscious mind.

42. The Freudian concept of a death instinct is called
    a. sublimation.
    b. ego-ideal.
    c. neurosis.
    d. Thanatos.

43. A(n) _____ is a form of mental illness in which a person is said to be out of touch with reality in some fundamental way.
    a. psychosis
    b. operant behavior
    c. sociopath
    d. neurosis

44. Freud stated that aggression was a response to
    a. anger.
    b. frustration.
    c. psychosis.
    d. neurosis.

45. According to Dollard, violence directed against something or someone who is not the source of the original frustration is known as
    a. repression.
    b. catharsis.
    c. Thanatos.
    d. displacement.

46. When crime leads to stress reduction as a result of internal changes in beliefs and value systems, it is known as _____ adaptation.
    a. alternative
    b. alloplastic
    c. antiplastic
    d. autoplastic

47. Which of the following behaviors is *not* aggression directed at one's self?
    a. Alcohol abuse
    b. Smoking
    c. Suicide
    d. They are all forms of self-directed aggression.

48. According to Gabriel Tarde's law of imitation, middle-class people would imitate
    a. lower-class people.
    b. other members of the middle class.
    c. upper-class individuals.
    d. no one.

49. Spanking a bad child is an example of a
    a. positive reward.
    b. negative reward.
    c. positive punishment.
    d. negative punishment.

50. Which of the following is *not* one of the forms of attachment identified by Bowlby?

    a. Secure
    b. Insecure
    c. Anxious avoidant
    d. Anxious resistant

51. When people resist temptations, they engage in which type of self-control?

    a. Control over one's emotional and mood states
    b. Control over the contents of the mind
    c. Impulse control
    d. Performance control

52. Which of the following is the definition of *insanity* under the Insanity Defense Reform Act?

    a. Because of a mental state or psychological condition the defendant was unable to resist committing the act.
    b. The defendant was suffering from a severe mental disease or defect and as a result was unable to appreciate the nature and quality or the wrongfulness of his acts.
    c. The defendant's actions were the product of mental disease or defect.
    d. The defendant cannot justly be held responsible for the criminal act in the face of any claims of insanity.

53. The _____ is a standard for judging legal insanity that considers whether a person was not able to resist committing the crime because of his or her mental state.

    a. *Durham* rule
    b. substantial capacity test
    c. irresistible-impulse test
    d. *Brawner* rule

54. The jury determines what constitutes insanity in states that use the

    a. *Durham* rule.
    b. substantial capacity test.
    c. irresistible-impulse test.
    d. *Brawner* rule.

Word Search Puzzle

```
X  U  L  W  J  Y  L  C  S  G  O  X  T  D  B  A  C  O  R  C  L  Y  S  O  L
S  H  K  C  X  B  Q  M  E  S  Z  S  E  L  F  C  O  N  T  R  O  L  U  D  K
U  G  T  C  H  S  O  T  J  Y  V  Y  V  E  M  K  E  W  W  W  Q  U  E  L  L
B  I  V  G  R  E  W  A  R  D  W  T  G  G  R  N  W  R  W  H  X  H  H  A  D
L  J  J  X  M  O  I  E  B  F  F  R  N  O  H  C  T  Z  O  M  C  H  C  I  U
I  W  N  A  T  P  M  F  J  P  N  G  S  C  K  P  Q  B  B  X  G  J  T  A  Z
M  L  F  X  W  L  C  Y  L  M  V  U  O  K  T  U  L  A  A  X  T  K  F  P  O
A  I  Y  N  S  F  S  C  H  I  Z  O  P  H  R  E  N  I  C  Q  S  A  I  U  B
T  X  U  C  O  Y  L  O  K  T  G  J  B  X  K  J  R  O  O  V  O  I  Y  E  M
I  O  Y  I  C  H  N  U  Z  O  V  A  C  Y  D  P  Q  J  W  R  N  H  W  C  D
O  P  P  D  I  O  W  S  U  K  Z  U  H  T  F  C  B  D  J  U  U  B  P  B  U
N  L  S  I  O  D  O  P  C  B  B  T  T  S  U  P  E  R  E  G  O  X  U  J  B
H  O  Y  I  P  C  K  S  O  D  X  O  L  K  D  Q  Y  Q  F  P  X  X  N  D  T
O  J  C  V  A  J  J  Y  N  U  J  P  T  S  D  A  E  J  H  S  P  R  I  R  H
N  Z  H  X  T  P  Y  C  D  D  T  L  H  Y  P  L  E  U  Y  Y  N  J  S  U  B
H  V  O  X  H  B  S  H  I  Z  R  A  A  S  S  L  Z  X  E  C  J  G  H  V  X
O  V  P  U  P  Y  C  O  T  I  U  S  N  B  Y  O  C  I  I  H  B  Q  M  C  U
E  W  A  N  A  N  Q  A  I  K  X  T  A  O  C  P  J  N  C  O  D  M  E  Q  M
I  V  T  K  X  Z  X  N  O  A  N  I  T  Y  H  L  O  S  R  T  O  G  N  Y  T
M  P  H  A  P  G  P  A  N  H  A  C  O  K  O  A  P  A  W  H  C  O  T  Q  N
P  O  V  D  G  D  E  L  I  U  Y  D  S  O  S  S  T  N  X  E  T  U  S  Y  X
T  I  M  J  H  U  I  Y  N  G  E  O  F  H  I  T  A  I  C  R  K  I  J  R  D
T  Z  V  Q  S  R  R  S  G  S  N  U  S  N  S  I  V  T  Q  A  Z  E  N  Y  T
N  M  H  Q  V  C  T  I  Y  A  O  L  X  Z  P  C  Z  Y  I  P  P  R  H  T  D
C  D  E  T  S  U  B  S  N  E  U  R  O  S  I  S  Y  O  U  Y  N  T  B  H  B
```

Alloplastic	Autoplastic	Conditioning	Ego	Id	Insanity
Neurosis	Psychoanalysis	Psychopath	Psychosis	Psychotherapy	Punishment
Reward	Schizophrenic	Self control	Sociopath	Sublimation	Superego
Thanatos					

Crossword Puzzle

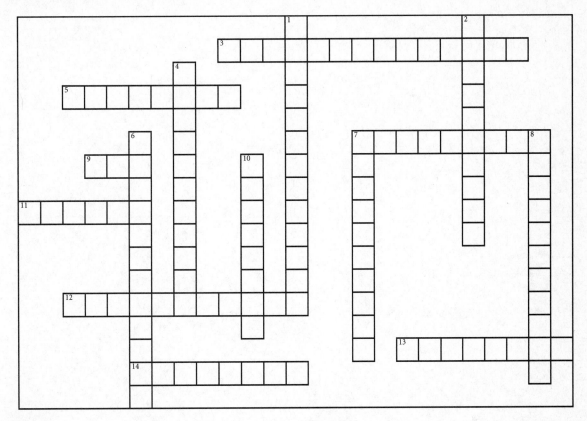

Across

3. Sigmund Freud's theory of human psychology.
5. The moral aspect of the personality.
7. A form of mental illness in which sufferers are said to be out of touch with reality.
9. The reality-testing part of the personality.
11. A desirable behavioral consequence likely to increase the frequency of the behavior.
12. _____ adaptation is a form of adjustment resulting from changes in the environment surrounding an individual.
13. A death wish.
14. A functional disorder of the mind or emotions.

Down

1. A mentally ill individual who is out of touch with reality and suffers from disjointed thinking.
2. An individual with a personality disorder manifested in aggressively antisocial behavior.
4. A person's ability to alter his or her own states and responses (two words).
6. A psychological principle that holds that the frequency of a behavior can be affected by reward or punishment.
7. Undesirable behavioral consequences likely to decrease the frequency of the behavior.
8. Symbolically substituting one aspect of consciousness for another.
10. Persistent mental disorder or derangement.

7 Social Structure Theories

Learning Outcomes

After reading this chapter, students should be able to:

- Explain the major principles of sociological theories and be able to identify three key sociological explanations for crime
- Show how the organization and structure of society may contribute to criminality, and explain what sociologists mean by the term *social structure*
- Identify three types of social structure theories and list the characteristics of each
- Identify modern-day crime control policies that reflect the social structure approach
- Assess the shortcomings of the social structure approach to understanding and preventing crime

Chapter Outline

Introduction
Major Principles of Sociological Theories
Social Structure Theories Defined
Types of Social Structure Theories
    Social Disorganization Theories
    Strain Theory
    Culture Conflict
Policy Implications of Social Structure Theories
Critique of Social Structure Theories

Chapter Summary

This chapter begins with an introduction to the general assumptions of sociological theories before focusing specifically on social structure theories—theories that explain crime as the result of the institutional structure of society. The three main types of social structure theories are social disorganization theories, strain theories, and culture conflict perspectives.

Social disorganization or ecological theories are associated with the Chicago School of criminology. Robert Park and Ernest Burgess viewed cities in terms of concentric zones, with Zone II, surrounding the city center, seen as the zone of transition. Clifford Shaw and Henry McKay applied concentric zone theory to crime and found that rates of offending remained fairly constant within the zone of transition despite the arrival of various new immigrant groups. The most important contribution of the ecological school to criminology is its claim that the community has a major influence on human behavior. Recently, the emergence of environmental criminology or the criminology of place has revived ecological approaches. The broken windows thesis holds that physical deterioration in an area leads to increased concerns for personal safety among area residents and to higher crime rates in that area. The concept of defensible space is used by the criminology of place as a mechanism for reducing the risk of crime.

Strain theories see delinquency as adaptive behavior committed in response to problems involving frustrating and undesirable social environments. Classic strain theory was developed by Robert K. Merton, who developed the concept of anomie as a disjunction between socially approved means to success and legitimate goals. He outlined five modes of adaptation, or combinations of goals and means, and suggested that innovation was the mode most likely to be associated with crime. Stephen Messner and Richard Rosenfeld developed a contemporary version of Merton's theory, based on the concept of relative deprivation, the economic and social gap between rich and poor living in close proximity to one another. General strain theory, developed by Robert Agnew, reformulated strain theory and suggested that delinquency is a coping mechanism that helps adolescents deal with socio-emotional problems generated by negative social reactions.

Culture conflict or cultural deviance theory suggests that crime results from a clash of values between differently socialized groups over what is acceptable or proper behavior. Thorsten Sellin suggests that conduct norms are acquired early in life through childhood socialization. Primary conflict occurs when there is a fundamental clash of cultures, while secondary conflict occurs when smaller cultures within the primary one clash. Subcultural theory emphasizes the contribution to crime made by variously socialized cultural groups within a primary culture. Walter Miller identified focal concerns or key values of delinquent subcultures that encourage delinquent behavior. On the other hand, Gresham Sykes and David Matza suggest that offenders use techniques of neutralization to negate the norms and values of the larger society and overcome feelings of guilt at committing criminal acts. Franco Ferracuti and Marvin Wolfgang postulated the existence of violent subcultures, which are built around values that support and encourage violence. Differential opportunity theory, developed by Richard Cloward and Lloyd Ohlin, combines elements of subcultural and strain theories to suggest that delinquency may result from the availability of illegitimate opportunities for success combined with the effective replacement of the norms of the primary culture with expedient subcultural rules. Albert Cohen also combined elements of strain theory and the subcultural perspective in his theory of reaction formation, which states that juveniles who are held accountable to middle-class norms and who cannot achieve these norms may reject middle-class goals and turn to delinquency instead.

The gangs studied by early researchers were involved primarily in petty theft, vandalism, and turf battles; modern gangs are involved in more serious and violent crimes and drug dealing. However, recent researchers draw a distinction between juvenile delinquency and gang-related violence, suggesting that they are ecologically distinct community problems.

Social structure theories have influenced social policy, through programs such as the Chicago Area Project, Mobilization for Youth, and the War on Poverty. The social structural perspective is closely associated with the social problems approach and negates the claims of the social responsibility perspective. The chapter discusses a number of critiques of each type of social structure theory.

Key Concepts

Anomie: A social condition in which norms are uncertain or lacking.

Broken windows thesis: A perspective on crime causation that holds that physical deterioration in an area leads to increased concerns for personal safety among area residents, and to higher crime rates in that area.

Chicago Area Project: A program focusing on urban ecology and originating at the University of Chicago during the 1930s, which attempted to reduce delinquency, crime, and social disorganization in transitional neighborhoods.

Chicago School of criminology: See **ecological theory.**

Conduct norms: Shared expectations of a social group relative to personal conduct.

Criminology of place: See **environmental criminology.**

Cultural transmission: The transmission of delinquency through successive generations of people living in the same area through a process of social communication.

Culture conflict theory: A sociological perspective on crime that suggests that the root cause of criminality can be found in a clash of values between variously socialized groups over what is acceptable or proper behavior.

Defensible space: The range of mechanisms that combine to bring an environment under the control of its residents.

Distributive justice: The rightful, equitable, and just distribution of rewards within a society.

Ecological theory: A type of sociological approach that emphasizes demographics (the characteristics of population groups) and geographics (the mapped location of such groups relative to one another) and sees the social disorganization that characterizes delinquency areas as a major cause of criminality and victimization. Also called *Chicago School of criminology.*

Environmental criminology: An emerging perspective that emphasizes the importance of geographic location and architectural features as they are associated with the prevalence of criminal victimization. (*Note*: as the term has been understood to date, environmental criminology is not the study of environmental crime but, rather, a perspective that stresses how crime varies from place to place.) Also called *criminology of place.*

Focal concerns: Key values of any culture, especially key values of a delinquent subculture.

General strain theory (GST):   A perspective that suggests that lawbreaking behavior is a coping mechanism that enables those who engage in it to deal with the socioemotional problems generated by negative social relations.

Illegitimate opportunity structure: Subcultural pathways to success that the wider society disapproves of.

Negative affective states: Adverse emotions that derive from the experience of strain, such as anger, fear, depression, and disappointment.

Reaction formation: The process by which a person openly rejects that which he or she wants or aspires to but cannot obtain or achieve.

Relative deprivation: A sense of social or economic inequality experienced by those who are unable, for whatever reason, to achieve legitimate success within the surrounding society.

Social disorganization: A condition said to exist when a group is faced with social change, uneven development of culture, maladaptiveness, disharmony, conflict, and lack of consensus.

Social disorganization theory: A perspective on crime and deviance that sees society as a kind of organism and crime and deviance as a kind of disease or social pathology. Theories of social disorganization are often associated with the perspective of social ecology and with the Chicago School of criminology, which developed during the 1920s and 1930s.

Social ecology: An approach to criminological theorizing that attempts to link the structure and organization of a human community to interactions with its localized environment.

Social life: The ongoing and (typically) structured interaction that occurs between persons in a society, including socialization and social behavior in general.

Social pathology: A concept that compares society to a physical organism and that sees criminality as an illness.

Social process: The interaction between and among social institutions, individuals, and groups.

Social structure: The pattern of social organization and the interrelationships between institutions characteristic of a society.

Social structure theory: A theory that explains crime by reference to some aspect of the social fabric. These theories emphasize relationships between social institutions and describe the types of behavior that characterize groups of people rather than individuals.

Sociological theory: A perspective that focuses on the nature of the power relationships that exist between social groups and on the influences that various social phenomena bring to bear on the types of behaviors that tend to characterize groups of people.

Strain theory: A sociological approach that posits a disjuncture between socially and subculturally sanctioned means and goals as the cause of criminal behavior. Also called *anomie theory*.

Subcultural theory: A sociological perspective that emphasizes the contribution made by variously socialized cultural groups to the phenomenon of crime.

Subculture: A collection of values and preferences that is communicated to subcultural participants through a process of socialization.

Technique of neutralization: A culturally available justification that can provide criminal offenders with the means to disavow responsibility for their behavior.

Questions for Review

1. What is the nature of sociological theorizing? What are the assumptions upon which sociological perspectives on crime causation rest? What three key sociological explanations for crime are discussed at the start of this chapter?
2. What do sociologists mean by the term *social structure*? How might the organization and structure of a society contribute to criminality?
3. What are the three types of social structure theories that this chapter describes? What are the major differences among them?
4. What are the policy implications of the theories discussed in this chapter? What kinds of changes in society and in government policy might be based on the theories discussed here? Would they be likely to bring about a reduction in crime?
5. What are the shortcomings of the social structure approach to understanding and preventing crime? Can these shortcomings be overcome?

Questions for Reflection

1. This book emphasizes a social problems versus social responsibility theme. Which of the theoretical perspectives discussed in this chapter best support the social problems approach? Which support the social responsibility approach? Why?
2. What do we mean by the term *ecological*? Do you believe that ecological approaches have a valid place in contemporary criminological thinking? Why?
3. How, if at all, does the notion of a "criminology of place" differ from more traditional ecological theories? Do you see the criminology-of-place approach as capable of offering anything new over traditional approaches? If so, what?
4. What is a violent subculture? Why do some subcultures seem to stress violence? How might participants in a subculture of violence be turned toward less aggressive ways?

Student Exercises

Activity #1

Obtain crime data from the UCR on crime in various neighborhoods in a large city near you. Plot the crime data on a county map. Do you see a pattern? Discuss whether concentric zone theory fits the crime distribution in your city.

Activity #2

Your instructor will place you into groups. Discuss the subcultures to which various members of the group belong. What norms and values of each subculture might conflict with the norms and values of the larger culture? Might any of these clashes lead to crime, delinquency, or deviance? How?

Criminology Today on the Web

www.gothicsubculture.com

This Web site provides a detailed description of the gothic subculture, a modern subculture present in American society.

http://social-sciences.uchicago.edu/ssdnews/fixing.html

This Web site provides a brief article on a recent study examining the broken windows thesis.

www.iir.com/nygc

This is the home page of the National Youth Gang Center.

www.ncjrs.gov/pdffiles1/ojjdp/fs200601.pdf

This link provides access to an OJJDP fact sheet with highlights of the 2004 National Youth Gang Survey.

www.iir.com/nygc/nygsa

This Web site presents a detailed analysis of the 2004 National Youth Gang Survey.

www.albany.edu/scj/jcjpc

This is the home page of the *Journal of Criminal Justice and Popular Culture*. Volume 3 contains an article on culture, crime, and cultural criminology.

Student Study Guide Questions

True or False

_____ 1. Sociological theories attempt to predict the specific behavior of a given individual.

_____ 2. According to Park and Burgess, the Loop, or central business district, is found in Zone II.

_____ 3. Data that describes the lives of city inhabitants is known as demographic data.

_____ 4. Classic strain theory was developed by Robert Merton.

_____ 5. One's perception of the rightful distribution of rewards depends on cultural expectations.

_____ 6. An individual experiencing personal deprivation is likely to feel socially isolated.

_____ 7. Culture conflict theory is incompatible with ecological criminology.

_____ 8. Most subcultures do not conform to the parameters of national culture.

_____ 9. According to Miller, subcultural crime and deviance are direct consequences of poverty and lack of opportunity.

_____ 10. Claiming that the authorities are corrupt is an example of the technique of neutralization known as condemning the condemners.

_____ 11. Techniques of neutralization allow delinquents to participate in crime without being fully alienated from the larger society.

_____ 12. For participants in violent subcultures, violence can be a way of life.

_____ 13. Participants in a violent subculture use techniques of neutralization to deal with feelings of guilt about their aggression

_____ 14. James Clarke suggests that the high rate of black underclass homicide in the United States may result from a black subculture of violence.

_____ 15. According to Cloward and Ohlin, a Type II youth wants wealth but does not want to be a member of the middle class.

_____ 16. Gang crime during the 1920s involved primarily vandalism and petty theft.

_____ 17. Most gangs are racially exclusive.

_____ 18. Gang homicides and delinquency appear to be ecologically distinct community problems.

Fill in the Blank

19. Social _____ theories stress the contribution of interpersonal relationships and a lack of self-control to crime.

20. Social _____ occurs when a group is faced with social change, uneven cultural development, maladaptiveness, disharmony, conflict, and lack of consensus.

21. According to Park and Burgess, Zone _____ was the commuter zone.

22. Criminology of place is also called _____ criminology.

23. _____ is a surrogate term for the range of mechanisms that combine to bring an environment under the control of its residents.

24. According to Robert K. Merton, _____ is a disjunction between socially approved means to success and legitimate goals.

25. The mode of adaptation that involves accepting the legitimate goals and the socially approved means of acquiring those goals is _____.

26. An individual who participates in socially desirable means but has little interest in achieving goals falls into the _____ mode of adaptation.

27. The social gap between rich and poor living in close proximity to one another is known as _____.

28. According to Thorsten Sellin, _____ conflict arises from a fundamental clash of cultures.

29. The concept of focal concerns was developed by _____.

30. The technique of neutralization best described by the belief that the insurance company will pay for the stolen car is _____.

31. According to Ferracuti and Wolfgang, the _____ involves legitimizing the use of violence as an appropriate way to resolve social conflicts.

32. The subcultural ethos of violence is most prominent in the _____ age group.

33. According to Cloward and Ohlin, participants in lower-class subcultures may be denied access to _____ opportunities.

34. According to Cloward and Ohlin, _____ is an effort to conform to subcultural norms and expectations.

35. According to Anderson, contemporary street code emphasizes the issue of _____.

36. Social structural theories negate the claims of the social _____ perspective.

Multiple Choice

37. Social _____ refers to institutional arrangements within society.
   a. structure
   b. life
   c. process
   d. pathology

38. Conflict theories see _____ as a fundamental cause of crime.
    a. social disenfranchisement
    b. a lack of self-control
    c. the strength of the social bond
    d. the nature of existing power relationships between social groups

39. According to Thomas and Znaniecki, increased crime rates among recent immigrants to America was due to social
    a. disorganization.
    b. conflict.
    c. pathology.
    d. ecology.

40. The idea of viewing cities in terms of concentric zones was developed by
    a. Clifford Shaw and Henry McKay.
    b. Robert Park and Ernest Burgess.
    c. W. I. Thomas and Florian Znaniecki.
    d. Steven Messner and Richard Rosenfeld.

41. According to Park and Burgess, Zone _____ contained mostly working-class tenements.
    a. II
    b. III
    c. IV
    d. V

42. Which of the following is *not* a characteristic of an urban transitional zone?
    a. Lower property values
    b. Impoverished lifestyles
    c. A general lack of privacy
    d. The presence of a significant amount of retail businesses

43. According to Merton, an innovator
    a. accepts both the legitimate goals and the socially approved means of acquiring those goals.
    b. rejects legitimate goals but accepts socially approved means.
    c. rejects both the legitimate goals and the socially approved means of acquiring those goals.
    d. accepts the legitimate goals but rejects the socially approved means of acquiring those goals.

44. According to general strain theory, strain occurs when which of the following events occurs?
    a. Someone tries to prevent you from achieving positively valued goals.
    b. Someone removes negatively valued stimuli.
    c. Someone presents you with positively valued stimuli.
    d. Someone helps you to achieve positively valued goals.

45. The book *Street Corner Society*, which studied the Italian slum known as
    "Cornerville," was written by

   a. William F. Whyte.
   b. Walter B. Miller.
   c. Frederic M. Thrasher.
   d. Gresham Sykes.

46. According to Miller, male involvement in fighting and sexual adventures while
    drinking represent which focal concern?

   a. Trouble
   b. Fate
   c. Autonomy
   d. Smartness

47. The technique of neutralization, which involves a young offender claiming that the
    unlawful acts were "not my fault," is known as

   a. denying injury.
   b. denying responsibility.
   c. appealing to higher loyalties.
   d. condemning the condemners.

48. The development of favorable attitudes toward the use of violence involves

   a. learned behavior.
   b. biological factors.
   c. psychological traits.
   d. frustration or strain.

49. It appears that certain forms of violence are more acceptable in the _____
    portion of the United States.

   a. Northeastern
   b. Southern
   c. Western
   d. Midwestern

50. The concept of "wholesale" and "retail" costs for homicide was developed by

   a. James Clark.
   b. Marvin Wolfgang.
   c. David Matza.
   d. Franklin Zimring.

51. According to Cloward and Ohlin, a Type _____ youth wants to desire wealth
    but not entry into the middle class.

   a. I
   b. II
   c. III
   d. IV

52. Reaction formation theory was developed by
    a. Albert Cohen.
    b. Thorsten Sellin.
    c. David Matza.
    d. Elijah Anderson.

53. _____ was based on the work of Cloward and Ohlin.
    a. Mobilization for Youth
    b. The Chicago Area Project
    c. The Welfare Reform Reconciliation Act
    d. Welfare-to-Work

54. Some researchers suggest that _____ theories fail to distinguish between the condition of social disorganization and the crimes that this condition is said to cause.
    a. ecological
    b. strain
    c. culture conflict
    d. subcultural

Word Search Puzzle

```
S  S  D  K  G  B  E  S  U  T  T  E  C  O  L  O  G  I  C  A  L  J  X  G  D
T  U  R  E  L  A  T  I  V  E  G  O  H  V  U  Y  R  B  R  G  X  Q  E  M  I
R  B  U  H  D  D  S  J  S  A  B  I  R  D  P  S  A  F  M  S  H  C  Y  T  S
U  C  H  C  Q  X  J  V  O  P  U  A  J  Q  T  B  X  G  X  O  F  T  Z  R  O
C  U  F  E  S  M  A  O  L  B  A  X  R  C  I  Z  D  R  E  C  P  T  E  A  R
T  L  I  I  T  N  E  U  T  R  A  L  I  Z  A  T  I  O  N  I  B  L  C  N  G
U  T  E  E  R  N  X  J  O  O  X  K  L  I  V  L  J  P  W  O  C  O  W  S  A
R  U  G  K  A  H  I  O  H  P  F  L  Q  V  Y  M  Y  Q  G  L  N  S  O  M  N
E  R  J  A  I  S  M  C  F  C  D  A  R  V  Q  S  A  S  W  O  W  S  C  I  I
B  E  N  N  N  R  J  N  P  S  T  H  E  P  N  H  R  V  U  G  F  M  Y  S  Z
F  T  G  O  Z  L  U  V  L  E  V  W  A  K  G  Z  Y  K  R  I  O  P  V  S  A
J  K  B  M  D  F  N  W  S  A  H  A  Z  Y  L  J  E  R  C  C  C  Q  V  I  T
T  Z  Y  I  F  Z  Y  Q  D  E  F  E  N  S  I  B  L  E  O  A  A  Q  A  O  I
T  Q  U  E  B  N  V  X  F  Q  B  I  S  N  C  F  E  P  N  L  L  O  B  N  O
C  H  B  O  D  I  S  T  R  I  B  U  T  I  V  E  G  W  F  R  C  L  M  D  N
A  R  B  P  I  N  O  X  P  H  K  W  M  M  M  D  F  G  L  O  O  E  B  E  F
N  E  D  U  Y  I  U  X  I  G  A  N  T  N  W  Z  Z  R  I  K  N  J  E  P  X
K  Q  Z  Q  P  S  V  Q  P  P  M  A  X  G  M  D  E  Y  C  R  C  Q  K  R  X
Z  I  Z  M  R  V  C  U  V  W  R  I  J  I  T  I  A  O  T  X  E  E  K  I  J
D  F  E  L  O  Y  H  A  T  O  L  R  L  R  P  M  U  L  U  Y  R  K  P  V  W
C  R  P  B  C  U  Q  W  R  Q  G  R  Z  L  M  U  C  D  T  B  N  B  S  A  V
V  V  G  T  E  V  W  Q  O  C  S  M  Z  W  H  C  R  N  H  S  S  I  B  T  I
F  C  L  G  S  E  Y  U  D  W  C  P  A  T  H  O  L  O  G  Y  D  H  J  I  E
F  N  D  G  S  C  P  J  N  J  Q  P  I  T  P  V  Z  X  K  M  D  D  N  O  J
K  H  V  B  L  V  Y  I  J  K  M  V  T  O  K  V  H  E  Y  H  D  T  X  N  O
```

Anomie	Conflict	Defensible	Deprivation	Disorganization	Distributive
Ecological	Focal concerns	Neutralization	Pathology	Process	Relative
Sociological	Strain	Structure	Subculture	Transmission	

Crossword Puzzle

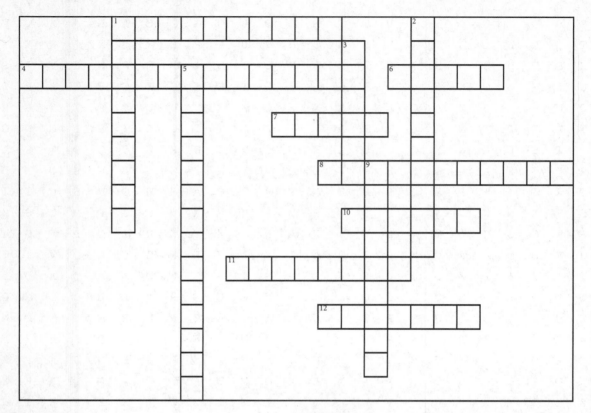

Across

1. A collection of values communicated to participants through a process of socialization.
4. Social _____ exists when a group is faced with social change, uneven culture development, and lack of consensus.
6. _____ concerns are the key values of a delinquent subculture.
7. Conduct _____ are shared expectations of a social group relative to personal conduct.
8. Relative _____ is the sense of inequality experienced by those unable to achieve legitimate success within the surrounding society.
10. A theory suggesting a disjuncture between socially sanctioned means and goals as the cause of crime.
11. _____ formation involves rejecting what one wants or aspires to but cannot have.
12. Social _____ is the interaction between and among social institutions, individuals, and groups.

Down

1. Social _____ is the interrelationships between institutions characteristic of a society.
2. Social disorganization is associated with the _____ school of criminology.
3. A social condition in which norms are uncertain or lacking.
5. Sykes and Matza proposed five techniques of _____.
9. Social _____ sees crime as an illness.

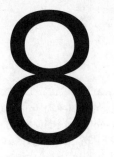

8 Theories of Social Process and Social Development

Learning Outcomes

After reading this chapter, students should be able to:

- Recognize how the process of social interaction contributes to criminal behavior
- Identify and distinguish among a number of social process perspectives
- Identify current social policy initiatives that reflect the social process approach
- Critique social process theories of criminality
- Identify and distinguish among a number of social development perspectives
- Explain the central concepts of social development theories
- Identify the policy implications of social development theories
- Assess the shortcomings of social development perspectives

Chapter Outline

Introduction
The Social Process Perspective
Types of Social Process Approaches
Learning Theory
Social Control Theory
Labeling Theory
Reintegrative Shaming
Dramaturgy
Policy Implications of Social Process Theories
Critique of Social Process Theories
The Social Development Perspective
Concepts in Social Development Theories
The Life Course Perspective
Laub and Sampson's Age-Graded Theory
Moffitt's Dual Taxonomic Theory
Farrington's Delinquent Development Theory
Evolutionary Ecology
Thornberry's Interactional Theory
Developmental Pathways
The Chicago Human Development Project
Policy Implications of Social Development Theories
Critique of Social Development Theories

Chapter Summary

This chapter begins with an introduction to social process theories or interactionist perspectives, which assume that everyone has the potential to violate the law, so that criminality is not an innate characteristic of certain individuals. The main types of social process theories are social learning theory, social control theory, labeling theory, the reintegrative shaming approach, and dramaturgy.

Learning theories suggest that crime, like all other types of behavior, is learned. One of the most influential learning theories is differential association, which was developed by Edwin Sutherland and which suggests that criminality is learned through a process of differential association with others who communicate criminal values and advocate the commission of crimes. Differential association-reinforcement theory adds the idea of reinforcement to Sutherland's theory; Robert Burgess and Ronald L. Akers integrated the concept of operant conditioning. Another theory building on Sutherland's work is Daniel Glaser's differential identification theory, which suggests that the process of differential association leads to an intimate personal identification with offenders, resulting in criminal acts.

Social control theories ask why people obey the laws instead of committing crimes. Containment theory, developed by Walter Reckless, suggests that individuals have control mechanisms, or containments, which protect them from crime; if these containments fail, people become vulnerable to criminal behavior. Howard Kaplan proposed the self-derogation theory of delinquency, which suggests that low self-esteem may promote delinquency, and that delinquent behavior may enhance self-esteem. Social bond theory, as proposed by Travis Hirschi, suggests that when the bond between an individual and a social group is weakened or broken, deviance and crime may result. Hirschi and Michael Gottfredson later proposed a general theory of crime that emphasized the lack of self-control as the key factor in explaining all types of crime. Charles Tittle's control-balance theory blends social bond and containment theory and includes the concept of a control ratio, which purports to predict not only the probability that one will engage in deviance but also the form that deviance will take.

Labeling theory focuses on society's reaction to deviance. Frank Tannenbaum developed the term *tagging* to explain how offenders become identified as bad and unredeemable after undergoing processing through the criminal justice system. The concepts of primary deviance (the offender's initial acts of deviance) and secondary deviance (continued acts of deviance) as developed by Edwin M. Lemert describe the development of a criminal career as a result of being tagged with the status of criminal. Howard Becker expanded on the labeling perspective, emphasizing that no act is intrinsically deviant, but must be so defined by society.

The concept of reintegrative shaming, developed by John Braithwaite, describes processes by which a deviant is labeled and sanctioned by society, but is then brought back into a community of conformity. According to Braithwaite, whereas stigmatic shaming destroys the moral bond between the offender and the community, reintegrative shaming strengthens the bond.

Finally, the dramaturgical perspective, developed by Erving Goffman, suggests that individuals play a variety of nearly simultaneous social roles that must be sustained in interaction with others. If discrediting information, or information that a person wants to hide, is revealed, the flow of interaction is disrupted and the nature of the performance may be changed substantially.

Social policy theories have influenced social policy through programs such as the Juvenile Mentoring Program, Preparing for the Drug Free Years, and the Montreal Preventive Treatment Program. The chapter discusses a number of critiques of each type of social policy theory.

Because the social development perspective focuses on human development on many levels, social development theories tend to be integrated theories. Major concepts in social development theories are discussed.

The life course perspective, developed by Robert J. Sampson and John Laub, focuses on the development of criminal careers over the life course and how these careers both start and finish. Laub and Sampson's age-graded theory involved reanalysis of data collected by Sheldon and Eleanor Glueck and emphasizes two key events in the life course (marriage and job stability) that seem to be particularly important in reducing the frequency of offending in later life.

Terrie Moffitt's dual taxonomic theory attempts to explain why, although adult criminality is almost always preceded by antisocial behavior during adolescence, most antisocial children do not become adult offenders. The theory discusses how positive developmental pathways may be fostered in adolescence. David P. Farrington and Donald J. West studied the issue of when offenders desist from crime. Other researchers using cohort analysis to study criminal careers include Marvin Wolfgang, who found that a small number of violent offenders were responsible for most of the crimes committed by the cohort. Lawrence E. Cohen and Richard Machalek developed the evolutionary ecology perspective, which attempts to explain how people acquire criminality, when and why they express it as crime, how individuals and groups respond to those crimes, and how this all interacts as a system evolving over time. Terence Thornberry's interactional theory integrates social control and social learning explanations of delinquency, suggesting that the fundamental cause of delinquency is a weakening of a person's bond to conventional society combined with the presence of an environment in which delinquency can be learned and in which rule-violating behavior can be positively rewarded. Thornberry says that delinquent peers are particularly important in providing the environment necessary for criminal behavior to develop. Because delinquents will seek out association with ever more delinquent groups if their delinquency continues to be rewarded, interactional theory sees delinquency as a process that unfolds over the life course.

A number of researchers are focusing on developmental pathways leading to criminality. The Program of Research on the Causes and Correlates of Delinquency is conducting a number of longitudinal studies of youth throughout their developmental years to understand the causes of delinquency and how it may be prevented. The Project on Human Development in Chicago Neighborhoods is a longitudinal study of how individuals, families, institutions, and communities evolve together and is tracing how criminal behavior evolves from birth to age 32.

Social development theories have influenced social policy. It is the foundation for the OJJDP's Comprehensive Strategy Program and for the Boys and Girls Clubs of America's Targeted Outreach program. The chapter discusses a number of critiques of social development theories.

Key Concepts

Cambridge Study in Delinquent Development: A longitudinal (life-course) study of crime and delinquency tracking a cohort of 411 boys born in London in 1953.

Cohort analysis: A social scientific technique that studies over time a population that shares common characteristics. Cohort analysis usually begins at birth and traces the development of cohort members until they reach a certain age.

Containment: Aspects of the social bond that act to prevent individuals from committing crimes and that keep them from engaging in deviance.

Containment theory: A form of control theory that suggests that a series of both internal and external factors contributes to law-abiding behavior.

Control ratio: The amount of control to which a person is subject versus the amount of control that person exerts over others.

Criminal career: The longitudinal sequence of crimes committed by an individual offender.

Desistance: The cessation of criminal activity or the termination of a period of involvement in offending behavior.

Differential association: The sociological thesis that criminality, like any other form of behavior, is learned through a process of association with others who communicate criminal values.

Differential identification theory: An explanation for crime and deviance that holds that people pursue criminal or deviant behavior to the extent that they identify themselves with real or imaginary people from whose perspective their criminal or deviant behavior seems acceptable.

Discrediting information: Information that is inconsistent with the managed impressions being communicated in a given situation.

Dramaturgical perspective: A theoretical point of view that depicts human behavior as centered around the purposeful management of interpersonal impressions. Also called *dramaturgy.*

Evolutionary ecology: An approach to understanding crime that draws attention to the ways people develop over the course of their lives.

General theory of crime: A perspective on crime, developed by Travis Hirschi and Michael Gottfredson, that asserts "that the operation of a single mechanism, low self-control, accounts for 'all crime, at all times'; [including] acts ranging from vandalism to homicide, from rape to white-collar-crime."

Human agency: The active role that people take in their lives; the fact that people are not merely subject to social and structural constraints but actively make choices and decisions based on the alternatives that they see before them.

Human development: The relationship between the maturing individual and his or her changing environment, as well as the social processes that the relationship entails.

Impression management: The intentional enactment of practiced behavior that is intended to convey to others one's desirable personal characteristics and social qualities.

Interactional theory: A theoretical approach to explaining crime and delinquency that blends social control and social learning perspectives.

Labeling: An interactionist perspective that sees continued crime as a consequence of limited opportunities for acceptable behavior that follow from the negative responses of society to those defined as offenders. Also, the process by which a negative or deviant label is imposed.

Learning theory: A perspective that places primary emphasis upon the role of communication and socialization in the acquisition of learned patterns of criminal behavior and the values that support that behavior.

Life course: Pathways through the age-differentiated life span. Also, the course of a person's life over time.

Life course criminology: A developmental perspective that draws attention to the fact that criminal behavior tends to follow a distinct pattern across the life cycle.

Moral enterprise: The efforts made by an interest group to have its sense of moral or ethical propriety enacted into law.

Persistence: Continuity in crime. Also, continual involvement in offending.

Primary deviance: Initial deviance often undertaken to deal with transient problems in living.

Prosocial bonds: Bonds between the individual and the social group that strengthens the likelihood of conformity. Prosocial bonds are characterized by attachment to conventional social institutions, values, and beliefs.

Project on Human Development in Chicago Neighborhoods (PHDCN):   An intensive study of Chicago neighborhoods employing longitudinal evaluations to examine the changing circumstances of people's lives in an effort to identify personal characteristics that may lead toward or away from antisocial behavior.

Reintegrative shaming: A form of shaming, imposed as a sanction by the criminal justice system, that is thought to strengthen the moral bond between the offender and the community.

Secondary deviance: Deviant behavior that results from official labeling and from association with others who have been so labeled.

Social bond: The link, created through socialization, between individuals and the society of which they are a part.

Social capital: The degree of positive relationships with others and with social institutions that individuals build up over the course of their lives.

Social control theory: A perspective that predicts that when social constraints on antisocial behavior are weakened or absent, delinquent behavior emerges. Rather than stressing causative factors in criminal behavior, control theory asks why people actually obey rules instead of breaking them.

Social development perspective: An integrated view of human development that examines multiple levels of maturation simultaneously, including the psychological, biological, familial, interpersonal, cultural, societal, and ecological levels.

Social process theory: A theory that asserts that criminal behavior is learned in interaction with others and that socialization processes that occur as the result of group membership are the primary route through which learning occurs. Also called the *interactionist perspective*.

Stigmatic shaming: A form of shaming, imposed as a sanction by the criminal justice system, that is thought to destroy the moral bond between the offender and the community.

Tagging: The process whereby an individual is negatively defined by agencies of justice. Also called *labeling*.

Total institutions: Facilities from which individuals can rarely come and go and in which communal life is intense and circumscribed. Individuals in total institutions tend to eat, sleep, play, learn, and worship (if at all) together.

Questions for Review

1. How does the process of social interaction contribute to criminal behavior?
2. What are the various social process perspectives discussed in this chapter? Describe each.
3. What kinds of social policy initiatives might be based on social process theories of crime causation?
4. What are the shortcomings of the social process perspective?
5. What are the various social development perspectives discussed in this chapter? Describe each.
6. What are the central concepts of social development theories? Explain each.

7. What kinds of social policy initiatives might be suggested by social development perspectives?
8. List and describe the various shortcomings of social development perspectives on criminality.

Questions for Reflection

1. This textbook emphasizes a social problems versus social responsibility theme. Which of the perspectives discussed in this chapter (if any) best support the social problems approach? Which (if any) support the social responsibility approach? Why?
2. This chapter describes both social process and social development perspectives. What are the significant differences between these two perspectives? What kinds of theories characterize each?
3. This chapter contains a discussion of the labeling process. Give a few examples of the everyday imposition of positive, rather than negative, labels. Why is it so difficult to successfully impose positive labels on individuals who were previously labeled negatively?
4. Do you believe that Erving Goffman's dramaturgical approach, which sees the world as a stage and individuals as actors upon that stage, provides any valuable insights into crime and criminality? If so, what are they?

Student Exercises

Activity #1

Your instructor will place you into groups and assign you one of the theories discussed in this chapter. Develop a crime reduction and/or prevention policy that is based on this theory. Explain how the theory justifies the policy and why you expect the policy to reduce or prevent crime.

Activity #2

According to Hirschi's social bond theory, four elements of a social bond work together to promote law-abiding behavior and prevent involvement in crime and delinquency: attachment, commitment, involvement, and belief. Explain how youth organizations, such as the Boy Scouts, Girl Scouts, and 4-H Clubs (or similar groups), work to strengthen these four elements of the social bond and encourage members to engage in normative behaviors.

Activity #3

Currently, there is considerable debate over the belief that violent video games may lead to criminal behavior among juveniles. Explain how this belief could be supported by the theories discussed in this chapter.

Criminology Today on the Web

www.sonoma.edu/cja/info/Edintro.html

This Web site was created in memory of Edwin Lemert, who died in 1996. It includes links to some of his articles and to an interview with him.

www.ncjrs.org/works

This site makes available a comprehensive report on the effectiveness of crime prevention that was mandated by Congress in 1996. It includes information on the relationship between various theories of crime causation and public policy, including many of the theories discussed in this chapter.

www.csudh.edu/dearhabermas/goffman.htm

This site includes resources relating to Erving Goffman's dramaturgy perspective.

www.crimetheory.com/Archive/Response/index.html

This site includes a discussion of various "social response" theories, including labeling theory.

www.aic.gov.au/rjustice/rise

The Australian Institute of Criminology has a Web site providing information on the Reintegrative Shaming Experiments project in Australia.

www.criminology.fsu.edu/crimtheory/farrington95.htm

This site provides the text of a lecture given by David P. Farrington, discussing findings from the Cambridge Study in Delinquent Development.

Student Study Guide Questions

True/False

_____ 1. Social process theories assume that criminality is an innate human characteristic.

_____ 2. Sutherland suggested that criminality occurs when there is a disjunction of socially approved goals and legitimate means.

_____ 3. According to Akers, differential reinforcement is also known as imitation.

_____ 4. According to Glaser, a role model must be an actual person.

_____ 5. According to Reckless, society provides individuals with meaningful roles and activities, which are an important factor in inner containment.

_____ 6. Delinquent behavior may enhance self-esteem.

_____ 7. Secondary deviance is usually undertaken to solve an immediate problem or to meet the expectations of one's subcultural group.

_____ 8. According to labeling theory, no act is intrinsically deviant.

_____ 9. According to labeling theory, deviance is the result of social processes involving the imposition of definitions.

_____ 10. The concept of reintegrative shaming emphasizes stigmatization and amplification of deviance.

_____ 11. Labeling theory has been criticized for failing to focus on secret deviants.

_____ 12. According to theories of social development, a critical transitional period occurs as a person moves from childhood to adulthood.

_____ 13. Criminality is relatively common during childhood.

_____ 14. Deceleration involves a reduction in the variety of offending.

_____ 15. Individuals with a history of conventional behavior will not begin offending in response to turning points.

_____ 16. Thornberry sees delinquency as a process that unfolds over the life course.

_____ 17. Children who do not develop adequate verbal coping skills are more likely to commit aggressive acts.

_____ 18. Simultaneous progression along multiple pathways to delinquency leads to higher rates of delinquency.

Fill in the Blank

19. Burgess and Akers added the concept of _____ to Sutherland's original idea of differential association.

20. According to Reckless, _____ containments are more important in preventing law violations.

21. According to Hirschi, a _____ has little or no attachment to society.

22. The _____ is the amount of control to which a person is subject versus the amount of control that person exerts over others.

23. Frank Tannenbaum popularized the term _____ to describe what happens to offenders following processing through the criminal justice system.

24. _____ deviance may be undertaken to solve an immediate problem.

25. A criminal who is caught in the act of committing a crime and who is then convicted and punished for the offense is an example of a(n) _____ deviant.

26. _____ shaming destroys the moral bond between the offender and the community.

27. _____ shaming condemns the crime but not the criminal.

28. _____ refers to the length of the criminal career.

29. A _____ is a pathway or line of development through life that is marked by a sequence of transitions.

30. The _____ type of activation involves an increased frequency of offending over time.

31. Elder's principle of _____ suggests that individuals construct their own life course through the choices they make.

32. Laub and Sampson's concept of _____ refers to the degree of positive relationships with other persons and with social institutions that people build up over the course of their lives.

33. According to Moffitt, _____ display constant patterns of misbehavior throughout life.

34. Moffit suggests that _____ offenders are led to offending primarily by structural disadvantages, such as status anxiety.

35. The _____ perspective on crime control was pioneered by Lawrence Cohen and Richard Machalek.

36. The first step on the overt pathway to delinquency occurs around age _____.

Multiple Choice

37. Social _____ theories assume that everyone has the potential to violate the law.
    a. development
    b. process
    c. structure
    d. disorganization

38. Edwin Sutherland developed
    a. dramaturgy.
    b. societal reaction theory.
    c. differential association theory.
    d. differential identification theory.

39. According to differential association theory, criminal behavior is
    a. inherited.
    b. learned.
    c. a function of culture conflict.
    d. none of the above

40. Burgess and Akers developed
    a. differential association theory.
    b. differential association-reinforcement theory.
    c. differential identification theory.
    d. none of the above

41. Rather than focusing on factors that cause criminal behavior, _____ theories examine factors that keep people from committing crimes.
    a. subcultural
    b. social control
    c. strain
    d. differential opportunity

42. The _____ element of a social bond refers to the amount of energy and effort put into activities with other people.
    a. attachment
    b. belief
    c. commitment
    d. involvement

43. The _____ element of a social bond refers to a shared value and moral system.
    a. attachment
    b. belief
    c. commitment
    d. involvement

44. Which of the following crimes would probably *not* be committed by an individual with a control deficit?
    a. Exploitation
    b. Sexual assault
    c. Submission
    d. Vandalism

45. The Women's Christian Temperance Union is an early example of
    a. tagging.
    b. labeling.
    c. moral enterprise.
    d. reintegrative shaming.

46. According to Becker's typology, a person who is punished for a crime he or she did not commit is a(n) _____ deviant.
    a. pure
    b. secret
    c. falsely accused
    d. innocent

47. Which of the following programs is based on concepts basic to social process theories?
    a. OJJDP's Comprehensive Strategy Program
    b. Targeted Outreach
    c. Mobilization for Youth
    d. OJJDP's Juvenile Mentoring Program

48. Life course criminology was given its name in a seminal book written by
    a. Michael Gottfredson and Travis Hirschi.
    b. Sheldon and Eleanor Glueck.
    c. Robert Sampson and John Laub.
    d. Terrie E. Moffitt.

49. Which of the following is *not* one of the three types of activation that are possible?
    a. Acceleration
    b. Diversification
    c. Stabilization
    d. Desistance

50. The dynamic process of _____ refers to the existence of a developmental sequence of activities that increase in seriousness over time.
    a. aggravation
    b. duration
    c. activation
    d. desistance

51. The _____ theory was developed by Laub and Sampson.
    a. age-graded
    b. dual taxonomic
    c. delinquent development
    d. evolutionary ecology

52. The _____ theory was developed by Terrie E. Moffitt.
    a. age-graded
    b. dual taxonomic
    c. delinquent development
    d. evolutionary ecology

53. Farrington and West found that offending tends to peak around age
    a. 13.
    b. 17.
    c. 25.
    d. 35.

54. According to the Causes and Correlates of Delinquency Program research, the _____ pathway to delinquency begins with behaviors such as frequent lying or shoplifting around age 10.
    a. overt
    b. authority conflict
    c. multiple disruption
    d. covert

Word Search Puzzle

```
O R C P Q B T U E J J E W A S G D I L X N O P V O
X V M J G M J Q Q T O W M R V J L B X I W K U O X
S N F Y S T I G M A T I C Z P I E Q S G C T I N K
V T X J H O C O H O R T O D U O A R Z A T Z T X L
V C W Q P E R S I S T E N C E N R E I B I Q G Z R
Q B A V M K Y R I G A P J L S F N J J I D P L Y G
S L K L S W O G N X W M G Z W E I S Y Q G Z I O F
R N J T T M O B T Z W H N U C R N H M G X F F Z C
C F O B I V Y X E F R Y U B Q Y G A H C H D E K Q
O N E E L V B O R T S I R V H Y U M Z O N R C Y E
N A M L Y V Y W A J O H M N M R G I E N A A O G S
T N D A B Y V Z C A C Q Y U K E Y N R T K M U D B
R H H B O T O W T A I S P D B I G G P A R A R G C
O Z Z E L H F A I R A A I I G N W O T I P T S H S
L Q H L Z P L K O G L G X S O T N I P N F U E X D
R B W I S P J L N H B X N C U E S D G M Z R P O C
A G V N X J R L A Y O S G R N G C B F E G G G W Y
T I K G L Y G L L Z N E H E O R M A X N D I X O Y
I Z U X U D S F G G D B Q D U A M T L T R C R G G
O D M B A I B S L E D E S I S T A N C E A A Y W S
M F J B H Q U P K L U D Q T M I F F S R R L J F K
F W S Z D P X R H X F F I I U V S K W P O V U T M
D P F D E V I A N C E F H N S E Q L S I V H M W V
Z A N O Z E N L C L W X D G Z D H F Z M G O S J H
N W U J L S R K T A G G I N G P Z C D V U X B X O
```

Cohort	Containment	Control ratio	Desistance	Deviance	Discrediting
Dramaturgical	Interactional	Labeling	Learning	Life course	Persistence
Reintegrative	Shaming	Social bond	Stigmatic	Tagging	

Crossword Puzzle

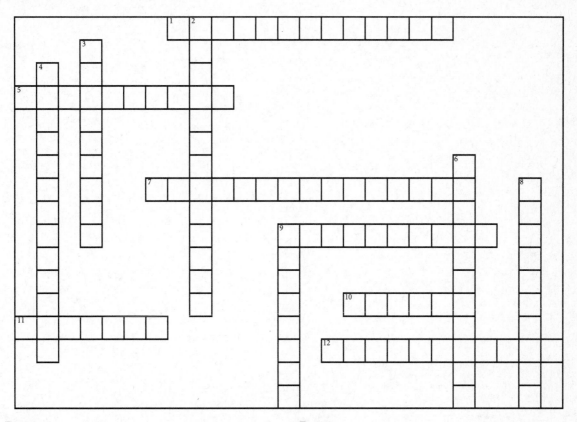

Across

1. A perspective that sees behavior as centered around the purposeful management of interpersonal impressions.

5. The link between individuals and the society of which they are a part (two words).

7. Efforts made by an interest group to have its sense of ethical propriety enacted into law (two words).

9. Pathways through the age-differentiated life span (two words).

10. A group of individuals sharing common social characteristics.

11. The process whereby an individual is negatively defined by agencies of justice.

12. _____ theory suggests that internal and external factors contribute to law-abiding behavior.

Down

2. A form of shaming that strengthens the moral bond between the offender and the community.

3. A form of shaming that destroys the moral bond between the offender and the community.

4. The degree of positive relationships with others that individuals build up over the course of their lives (two words).

6. Continual involvement in offending.

8. The cessation of criminal activity.

9. The process by which one is negatively defined by agencies of justice.

9 Social Conflict Theories

Learning Outcomes

After reading this chapter, students should be able to:

- Enumerate and describe three analytical perspectives on law and social order
- Describe the central tenants of radical criminology and critique that theory
- Identify and describe at least three emerging conflict theories that purport to explain crime
- Describe the crime control policy implications of social conflict theories

Chapter Outline

Chapter Summary

This chapter begins with a discussion of three analytical perspectives: consensus, pluralist, and conflict. The consensus perspective is based on the premise that most members of society agree on what is right and wrong and share a set of core values. This perspective assumes that the criminal law reflects the collective will of the people and serves everyone equally, and believes that criminals are unique. The pluralistic perspective assumes that there is a variety of different viewpoints, values, and beliefs, but that most individuals agree on the usefulness of law as a formal means of dispute resolution, so that the law is a peace-keeping tool used to resolve conflict. The conflict perspective holds that there is no consensus on what is right and wrong, that conflict is a fundamental aspect of social life, and that the law is a tool of the powerful that is used to maintain their power.

The conflict perspective is based on the writings of Karl Marx, who believed that conflict was inevitable in any capitalist society. The six key elements of the conflict perspective are outlined, and the concept of social class, a topic central to the conflict perspective, is discussed. Other early conflict theorists include George Vold, who described crime as the result of political conflict between groups, Ralf Dahrendorf, who considered conflict to be a normal part of any society, and Austin Turk, who considered crime a natural consequence of intergroup conflict.

Modern radical criminology suggests that crime causes are rooted in social conditions empowering the wealthy and politically well-organized and disenfranchising those less fortunate. William Chambliss, a modern radical thinker, emphasizes the power gap between the powerful and powerless as helping to create crime. Richard Quinney outlined six Marxist principles for an understanding of crime. He stated that crime is inevitable under capitalist conditions and that the problem of crime can only be solved by the development of a socialized society.

A distinction is made between critical criminology, which is a way of critiquing social relationships that lead to crime, and radical criminology, which is a proactive call for radical change in the social conditions leading to crime. Most modern radical-critical criminologists focus on promoting a gradual transition to socialized forms of government activity. Critiques of radical-critical criminology include its overemphasis on methods at the expense of well-developed theory, its failure to recognize the existence of a fair degree of public consensus about the nature of crime, and its inability to explain low crime rates in some capitalist countries or the problems existing in communist countries.

There are a variety of new innovative conflict theories. Left-realist criminology portrays crime in terms understandable to those most affected by it, shifting the focus to a pragmatic assessment of crime and the needs of victims. Key scholars include Walter DeKeseredy and Jock Young. A key principle of left realism is that radical ideas must be translated into realistic social policies. Critiques of left-realist criminology include the claim that it represents more of an ideological emphasis than a theory and the belief that realist criminologists build upon existing theoretical frameworks but rarely offer new testable propositions or hypotheses. Feminist criminology attempts to include gender awareness in the thinking of mainstream criminologists, pointing out inequities inherent in patriarchal forms of thought. Early researchers include Freda Adler and Rita J. Simon, who suggested that gender differences in crime rates were due to socialization, not biology. However, despite increased gender equality, the criminal behavior of men and women has not become more similar. Key contemporary theorists include Kathleen Daly and Meda Chesney-Lind, who are concerned about androcentricity in criminology. There are several schools of feminist thought, including radical feminism, liberal feminism, and social feminism, as well as a perspective developed by women of color emphasizing feminism's sensitivity to the interplay of gender, class, and race oppression. John Hagan developed power-control theory, which suggests that the social distribution of criminality is passed on by the family. Modern feminist thinkers suggest social policies such as increasing controls over male violence towards women, creating alternatives for women facing abuse, and the protection of children. Critiques of feminist theory suggest that it may be a theory in formation, rather than a completely developed theory of crime. Some critics argue that a feminist criminology is impossible, although feminist thought may inform criminology.

Postmodern criminology applies understandings of social change inherent in postmodern philosophy to criminological theorizing and to issues of crime control. Much is deconstructionist, challenging existing criminological perspectives and working toward replacing them with perspectives more relevant to the postmodern era. Two key postmodern criminologists are Stuart Henry and Dragan Milovanovic, who focus on constitutive criminology, claiming that crime and crime control are constructions produced through a social process involving the offender, victim, and society and stating that crime should be understood as an integral part of society. Critics of postmodern theory claim that the terminology is vaguely defined and the approaches are often incoherent and confusing, and that postmodernism challenges traditional theories but fails to offer viable alternatives for crime prevention and control.

Peacemaking criminology is a new form of postmodernism that suggests citizens and social control agencies need to work together to alleviate social problems and reduce crime. Key theorists include Harold Pepinsky and Richard Quinney, who suggest that the problem of crime control is not "how to stop crime" but rather "how to make peace." Peacemaking emphasizes a peace model of crime control, focusing on ways of developing a shared consensus on critical issues such as crime. Programs such as dispute resolution are based on the participatory justice principle. Restorative justice is a social movement stressing healing over retribution. Peacemaking criminology has been criticized as being naïve and utopian and for failing to recognize the realities of crime control and law enforcement.

Finally, convict criminology is the newest radical paradigm to emerge. It is primarily a body of writings and musings on criminology by convicted felons and ex-inmates who have acquired academic credentials or who are associated with credentialed others. They primarily use ethnographic methods to study criminology and have produced a number of recommendations for improving the justice system. Critics suggest that having been in prison may distort one's view of the field rather than enhance it and are concerned that personal experience does not give one the entire picture needed to understand a phenomenon.

Social conflict theory suggests that reducing conflict will lead to a reduction in crime rates. The various schools of thought have different views of how to reduce conflict, ranging from the use of conflict resolution to the replacement of the existing capitalist system with a socialist economic structure.

Key Concepts

Androcentricity: A single-sex perspective, as in the case of criminologists who study only the criminality of males.

Bourgeoisie: In Marxian theory, the class of people who own the means of production.

Conflict perspective: An analytical perspective on social organization that holds that conflict is a fundamental aspect of social life itself and can never be fully resolved.

Consensus model: An analytical perspective on social organization that holds that most members of society agree about what is right and what is wrong and that the various elements of society work together in unison toward a common vision of the greater good.

Convict criminology: A new analytical paradigm consisting of writings on the subject matter of criminology by convicted felons and ex-inmates who have acquired academic credentials, or who are associated with credentialed others.

Critical criminology: See **radical criminology**.

Deconstructionist theory: A postmodernist perspective that challenges existing criminological theories in order to debunk them and that works toward replacing traditional ideas with concepts seen as more appropriate to the postmodern era.

Feminist criminology: A self-conscious corrective model intended to redirect the thinking of mainstream criminologists to include gender awareness.

Gender gap: The observed differences between male and female rates of criminal offending in a given society, such as the United States.

Instrumental Marxism: A perspective that holds that those in power intentionally create laws and social institutions that serve their own interests and that keep others from becoming powerful.

Left realism: A conflict perspective that insists on a pragmatic assessment of crime and its associated problems. Also called *realist criminology*.

Left-realist criminology: An approach to the subject matter of criminology based on ideas inherent in the perspective of left realism.

Liberal feminism: A perspective that holds that the concerns of women can be incorporated within existing social institutions through conventional means and without the need to drastically restructure society. Criminal laws, such as the Violence Against Women Act, for example, have been enacted in order to change the legal structure in such a way that it becomes responsive to women's issues.

Marxist criminology: See **radical criminology**.

Participatory justice: A relatively informal type of criminal justice case processing that makes use of local community resources rather than requiring traditional forms of official intervention.

Patriarchy: The tradition of male dominance.

Peace model: An approach to crime control that focuses on effective ways for developing a shared consensus on critical issues that could seriously affect the quality of life.

Peacemaking criminology: A perspective that holds that crime control agencies and the citizens they serve should work together to alleviate social problems and human suffering and thus reduce crime.

Pluralist perspective: An analytical approach to social organization that holds that a multiplicity of values and beliefs exists in any complex society but that most social actors agree on the usefulness of law as a formal means of dispute resolution.

Postmodern criminology: A brand of criminology that developed following World War II and that builds on the tenets inherent in postmodern social thought.

Power-control theory: A perspective that holds that the distribution of crime and delinquency within society is to some degree founded upon the consequences that power relationships within the wider society hold for domestic settings and for the everyday relationships among men, women, and children within the context of family life.

Proletariat: In Marxist theory, the working class.

Radical criminology: A perspective that holds that the causes of crime are rooted in social conditions that empower the wealthy and the politically well organized but disenfranchise those less fortunate. Also called *critical criminology*; *Marxist criminology*.

Radical feminism: A perspective that holds that any significant change in the social status of women can be accomplished only through substantial changes in social institutions such as the family, law, and medicine. Radical feminism argues, for example, that the structure of current legal thinking involves what is fundamentally a male perspective, which should be changed to incorporate women's social experiences and points of view.

Restorative justice: A postmodern perspective that stresses "remedies and restoration rather than prison, punishment and victim neglect."

Social class: Distinctions made between individuals on the basis of important defining social characteristics.

Socialist feminism: A perspective that examines social roles and the gender-based division of labor within the family, seeing both as a significant source of women's subordination within society. This perspective calls for a redefinition of gender-related job status, compensation for women who work within the home, and equal pay for equal work regardless of gender.

Structural Marxism: A perspective that holds that the structural institutions of society influence the behavior of individuals and groups by virtue of the type of relationships created. The criminal law, for example, reflects class relationships and serves to reinforce those relationships.

Questions for Review

1. What three analytical perspectives on law and social order are described in this chapter?
2. What are the central tenants of radical criminology? What are its shortcomings?
3. What three emerging conflict perspectives discussed in this chapter purport to explain crime and criminality?
4. What are the crime control implications of social control theory?

Questions for Reflection

1. This book emphasizes a social problems versus social responsibility theme. Which of the theoretical perspectives discussed in this chapter (if any) best support the social problems approach? Which (if any) support the social responsibility approach? Why?
2. Explain the differences among the consensus, pluralistic, and conflict perspectives. Which comes closest to your way of understanding society? Why?
3. What is Marxist criminology? How, if at all, does it differ from radical criminology? From critical criminology?
4. Does the Marxist perspective hold any significance for contemporary American society? Why?
5. What are the fundamental propositions of feminist criminology? How would feminists change the study of crime?
6. What does it mean to say that traditional theories of crime need to be "deconstructed"? What role does deconstructionist thinking play in postmodern criminology?

Student Exercises

Activity #1

Your instructor will place you into groups and assign you one of the radical-critical theories discussed in this chapter. Develop a crime reduction and/or prevention policy that is based on this theory. Explain how the theory justifies the policy and why you expect the policy to reduce or prevent crime.

Activity #2

Locate a program in your community that emphasizes restorative justice (for example, an alternative dispute resolution program). Describe the program and how it works to reintegrate offenders back into the community after they have been punished by the criminal justice system. Discuss the success/failure rate of the program.

Criminology Today on the Web

www.critcrim.org

This is the Web site for the American Society of Criminology's Critical Criminology Division.

http://online.anu.edu.au/polsci/marx/marx.html

This site, the Marxism Page, is devoted to Karl Marx and includes a considerable amount of information on Marxism.

http://peacemakingandcrime.blogspot.com

This is a blog focusing on the peacemaking model of criminal justice, run by Dr. John Fuller, professor of criminology and sociology at the State University of West Georgia.

www.restorativejustice.org

This site is devoted to the topic of restorative justice.

www.umsl.edu/~rkeel/200/powcontr.html

This Web site provides a discussion of power-control and feminist theories.

Student Study Guide Questions

True/False

_____ 1. According to the pluralist perspective, law violators suffer from some lapse that makes them unable to participate in the widespread agreement on values and behavior.

_____ 2. According to Roscoe Pound, the law is designed to meet the needs of everyone living together in society.

_____ 3. According to the pluralistic perspective, the legal system is value neutral.

_____ 4. According to the pluralistic perspective, the legal system focuses primarily on the needs of the rich and politically powerful.

_____ 5. Karl Marx believed that the natural outcome of the struggle between the proletariat and the bourgeoisie would be the overthrow of a communistic social order.

_____ 6. According to Ralf Dahrendorf, conflict is ubiquitous.

_____ 7. Instrumental Marxism sees the criminal law and the criminal justice system as tools used to keep the poor disenfranchised.

_____ 8. Most radical-critical criminologists today are focusing on a sudden and total reversal of existing political arrangements within the United States.

_____ 9. One criticism of radical-critical criminology is its failure to recognize that there is a fair degree of public consensus about the nature of crime.

_____ 10. Left realism is more conservative than traditional Marxist criminology.

_____ 11. *Women in Crime* was written by Freda Adler.

_____ 12. According to early feminist criminology, as gender equality increased, male and female criminality would take on similar characteristics.

_____ 13. According to feminist thought, gender is a natural fact.

_____ 14. Power-control theory would suggest that a paternalistic model of family structure would result in higher levels of female delinquency.

_____ 15. According to feminist criminologists, criminal laws reflect traditionally male ways of organizing the social world.

_____ 16. Gender differences in crime appear to exist in every society that has been systematically studied.

_____ 17. Adversarial court proceedings are based on the principle of participatory justice.

_____ 18. Peacemaking criminologists primarily envision positive change on an individual level.

Fill in the Blank

19. According to the _____ perspective, the law serves all people equally.

20. According to the _____ perspective, the law is a peacekeeping tool that allows agencies within the government to settle disputes effectively.

21. The _____ are the capitalists, according to Marx.

22. Level of education is an example of a(n) _____ characteristic.

23. George Vold described crime as the product of _____ conflict between groups.

24. According to Ralf Dahrendorf, the _____ of conflict would be surprising and abnormal.

25. According to _____ Marxists, the legal system keeps control in the hands of those who are already powerful.

26. _____ criminology is a proactive call for change in the social conditions leading to crime.

27. _____ has been credited with popularizing left realism in North America.

28. According to _____, radical ideas must be translated into realistic social policies.

29. _____ is a term referring to male dominance.

30. The book *Women and Crime* was written by _____.

31. According to _____ theory, family class structure affects the social distribution of delinquency.

32. Postmodern criminological theories are sometimes called _____ theories.

33. A central feature of _____ criminology is the assertion that individuals both shape and are shaped by their world.

34. The _____ model of crime control focuses on effective ways for developing a shared consensus on critical issues that have the potential to seriously affect the quality of life.

35. Alternative dispute resolution programs play an important role in _____ perspectives.

36. Miami-Dade County's drug court is an example of a(n) _____ program.

Multiple Choice

37. The work *The Communist Manifesto* was written by
    a. Karl Marx and Friedrich Engels.
    b. Dragan Milovanovic.
    c. Raymond J. Michalowski.
    d. Richard Quinney.

38. The idea that those who violate the law represent a unique subgroup with some distinguishing feature is a key principle of the _____ perspective.
    a. pluralist
    b. conflict
    c. consensus
    d. radical

39. According to Karl Marx, the _____ are the exploited working class who are without power.
    a. proletariat
    b. bourgeoisie
    c. petit bourgeoisie
    d. materialists

40. Which of the following is *not* an ascribed characteristic?
    a. Race
    b. Gender
    c. Income
    d. Family background

41. According to George Vold, as intergroup conflict intensifies, the loyalty of individual members to their groups
    a. increases.
    b. decreases.
    c. stays about the same.
    d. Vold did not discuss this topic.

42. The conflict view of crime as a manifestation of denied needs and values was espoused by
    a. Ralf Dahrendorf.
    b. Willem Bonger.
    c. George Vold.
    d. Karl Marx.

43. According to Ralf Dahrendorf, constructive change increases _____ within society.
    a. cohesiveness
    b. tension
    c. conflict
    d. stasis

44. The book *Criminality and Legal Order* was written by
    a. Ralf Dahrendorf.
    b. Willem Bonger.
    c. George Vold.
    d. Austin Turk.

45. According to Richard Quinney, the state is organized to serve the interests of the
    a. proletariat.
    b. working class.
    c. dominant economic class.
    d. petty bourgeoisie.

46. Richard Quinney suggests that the problem of crime will be solved only by the creation of
    a. a class structure.
    b. a socialist society.
    c. hedonistic values.
    d. a capitalist society.

47. Which of the following books was written by Jeffrey Reiman?
    a. *Class, State, and Crime*
    b. *Law, Order and Power*
    c. *The Rich Get Richer and the Poor Get Prison*
    d. *Class and Class Conflict in Industrial Society*

48. Modern radical criminologists have escalated their demands for
    a. an end to police misconduct.
    b. increased use of capital punishment.
    c. mandatory sentencing guidelines.
    d. increased funding for new prison construction.

49. _____ was an early feminist criminologist.
    a. Meda Chesney-Lind
    b. Rita Simon
    c. Kathleen Daly
    d. John Hagan

50. A demand for the elimination of the traditional divisions of power and labor between the sexes would probably come from a(n) _____ feminist.
    a. socialist
    b. radical
    c. liberal
    d. alternative (women of color)

51. The alternative feminist framework developed by women of color was identified by
    a. Rita J. Simon.
    b. Kathleen Daly.
    c. Meda Chesney-Lind.
    d. Sally S. Simpson.

52. Stuart Henry and Dragan Milovanovic are known for their development of _____ criminology.
    a. constitutive
    b. anarchic
    c. peacemaking
    d. semiotic

53. Which of the following is a criticism of postmodern criminology?
    a. It is a theory in formation rather than a completely developed theory of crime.
    b. Postmodernists build upon existing theoretical frameworks but rarely offer new testable propositions or hypotheses.
    c. Postmodernists use terminology that is only vaguely defined.
    d. It is naïve and utopian.

54. A peace model is based on
    a. cooperation.
    b. retribution.
    c. just deserts.
    d. All of the above

Word Search Puzzle

```
Q Z L Z N P Q T C L U X I T S U U Y H Z N B T L P
C Y K U J K U I D B C O N S E N S U S G L V I B O
B O U R G E O I S I E R T M T R V T V S W J N R Q
I J O F W K R V R A Q Y X K W B E P O Q A M S I D
D E C O N S T R U C T I O N I S T R G N N Y T W A
L V P X V L B U E J B J R W Z R Y O B P D Y R G H
Y O L K K E I F M L V O M R T F L A A R N U P I
A Z Q X Y M T I L S F L X E R C I E N T O C M E O
W E N T T G Q T V U D X S P N U T T Q R C X E A T
Z K X Z K S Q U P W C A R V M S X A S I E T N C F
C Z T D K U Y B S V J S K O H C N R A A N B T E E
G L D G G U X C R T T J Y N I R Y I H R T E A M M
E I I C O N V I C T Z F A L Z I K A X C R G L A I
P O S T M O D E R N F C G L O T V T Z H I T U K N
N U G I W T I S Z X B I D P T I O S F Y C X Y I I
C H I L V Q V V F V G L M L G C H I E H I X H N S
S M I H I X L B G G P A U U V A K E X N T F R G T
G K L R A D I C A L N V U R Q L N N I Y Y B R M H
I R A Q B T D Z L Y M D X A A H L X N M T P T T Q
B S M X Y F K R Q C O N F L I C T N D B X S Z V H
F Z C B H B O K V V Y P Q R I R E G C E Q Q I V G R
K X E C X F O F Y U R F T S T J J G Y P J U R T A
A F R I R E O Y Z H Q L J T A A Z E R X N W R Q D
K I I N X M B Q Q T Y F C I D H U B Z O I V Z J B
L Q E A O C H O G W C E A C S T X S W K J X H W V
```

Androcentricity	Bourgeoisie	Conflict	Consensus	Convict
Critical	Deconstructionist	Feminist	Instrumental	Patriarchy
Peacemaking	Pluralistic	Postmodern	Proletariat	Radical

Crossword Puzzle

Across

1. _____ justice is a postmodern perspective stressing remedies over prison and punishment.

5. A model suggesting that society generally agrees on what is right and wrong.

6. The feminist perspective that examines social roles and the gender-based division of labor within the family.

10. A single-sex perspective, such as criminologists who only study the criminality of males.

11. The observed differences between male and female rates of criminal offending in a society (two words).

12. Distinctions made between individuals based on important defining social characteristics (two words).

13. The perspective that holds that citizens and crime control agencies should work together to alleviate social problems and human suffering and thus reduce crime.

14. The feminist perspective suggesting that eliminating male dominance should reduce crime rates for women.

15. _____ Marxism holds that social institutions influence individual and group behavior because of the type of relationships created.

Down

2. _____ Marxism sees the criminal law as a tool used by the powerful to control the poor.

3. _____ criminology is a paradigm involving writings by convicted felons and ex-inmates.

4. In Marxian theory, the class of people who own the means of production.

7. A conflict perspective that insists on a pragmatic assessment of crime and its associated problems (two words).

8. In Marxian theory, the working class.

9. The tradition of male dominance.

10

Crimes against Persons

Learning Outcomes

After reading this chapter, students should be able to:

- Explain the general nature of typologies and describe various typologies of violent crime
- Identify the key issues in explaining patterns of homicide
- Identify the key issues in explaining as well as preventing the crimes of rape and child sexual abuse
- List the different kinds of robbery and describe the criminal careers of robbers
- Identify various kinds of assault, and describe what is known about intimate partner violence
- Define *workplace violence* and tell what is known about the offense
- Explain the major patterns of stalking and identify the different types of stalkers

Chapter Outline

Chapter Summary

This chapter discusses various types of violent crime in America, including homicide, rape, robbery, assault, workplace violence, stalking, and terrorism. Homicide research focuses on two main theoretical frameworks, using subcultural and structural explanations to understand variations in homicide offending. Examinations of the relationship between the victim and the offender have found that homicides frequently involve family members, friends, or acquaintances. Victim precipitation studies characteristics of victims that may have precipitated their victimization, although the focus is not on "blaming the victim" for the crime. Factors such as weapons availability and the use of alcohol and drugs may also be associated with homicide. Gang membership may influence homicides; research shows several differences between homicides involving gang and nongang members. Serial and mass murder are also discussed, and several typologies are presented

It is difficult to measure the extent of rape in this country because the figures vary depending on the source used. Because many rapes are not reported to the police, official statistics frequently underestimate the extent of rape in the United States today. Rape myths, which are false assumptions about rape, inhibit reporting of this crime. The common law definition of *rape*, which was recognized in the United States until the 1970s, did not recognize male victims or rape within marriage; common law rules of evidence required victims to demonstrate physical resistance and to have some form of corroboration that the rape occurred. Rape law reform is designed to make the legal understanding of rape similar to that of other violent crime. All states have made significant changes in the common law crime of rape, although the impact of these reforms varies widely. The majority of rapes involve victims and offenders who are acquainted. College and university campuses typically have a high incidence of rape. Law reform has eliminated the marital exemption for rape and the text presents a typology of men who rape their wives. Same-sex rape is common in both male and female correctional institutions, although the patterns vary: rape within female prisons primary involves the attack of inmates by male staff while in male prisons the assault involves only inmates. Theoretical perspectives surrounding rape include feminist perspectives, the psychopathological perspective, Baron and Strauss's integrated theory of rape, and evolutionary and biological perspectives. Various typologies of rapists have been developed, often based on offender motivation. Child sexual abuse includes a variety of offenses in which an adult engages in sexual activity with a minor, exploits a minor for purposes of sexual gratification, or exploits a minor sexually for purposes of profit. Sexual crimes against juveniles are underreported. Several typologies have been developed to classify child sex offenders.

Robbery is considered a violent crime because the use or threat of force is involved in the crime. There is a high potential for injury and even death for robbery victims. Most robbers are generalists; few specialize in robbery alone. Many robbers are motivated by direct financial need. Offenders specializing in street robbery frequently target other criminals, especially lower-level drug dealers, both because of the opportunity to obtain not only money but also drugs, and because these victims would be less likely to report their victimization to the police. With the exception of rape, robbery may be the most gender-differentiated serious crime in the United States, as the vast majority of offenders are male. Male and female offenders differ significantly in how they carry out street robberies, although the primary motivation for both is economic.

Assault is the most frequent violent crime and is similar psychologically, although not legally, to homicide. The offender profiles for homicide and assault are extremely similar. The majority of assaults involve victims and offenders who are known to each other, frequently in a familial or intimate relationship. Research into familial violence has been hindered by the belief that the family is a private institution. NIBRS data on family assaults shows some differences from aggravated assaults generally. Intimate partner assault involves assaultive behavior between individuals involved in an intimate relationship. The majority of victims are female, although men may also be victims.

Workplace violence, which includes a variety of violent crimes committed against persons who are at work or on duty, is a significant problem in America today. There is a variety of job-related factors that increase the risk of workplace violence and a number of prevention strategies that may be employed. All workplace violence falls into four broad categories.

Stalking involves ongoing patterns of behavior that cause victims to fear for their personal safety. All states, and the federal government, currently have antistalking laws. Stalking behaviors can include making telephone calls, following the victim, sending letters, making threats, vandalizing property, or watching the victim. Data on the extent of stalking is available from the National Violence Against Women Survey. The majority of victims are women and the majority of stalkers are men. Women are more likely to be stalked by an intimate partner while men are more likely to be stalked by strangers or acquaintances. Cyberstalking involves using electronic communication, such as e-mail or the Internet, to harass individuals.

Key Concepts

Acquaintance rape: Rape characterized by a prior social, though not necessarily intimate or familial, relationship between the victim and the perpetrator.

Crime typology: A classification of crimes along a particular dimension, such as legal categories, offender motivation, victim behavior, or the characteristics of individual offenders.

Cyberstalking: An array of high-technology related activities in which an offender may engage to harass or "follow" individuals, including e-mail and the Internet.

Exposure-reduction theory: A theory of intimate homicide that claims that a decline in domesticity, accompanied by an improvement in the economic status of women and a growth in domestic violence resources, explains observed decreases in intimate-partner homicide.

Expressive crime: A criminal offense that results from acts of interpersonal hostility, such as jealousy, revenge, romantic triangles, and quarrels.

Institutional robbery: Robbery that occurs in commercial settings, such as convenience stores, gas stations, and banks.

Instrumental crime: A goal-directed offense that involves some degree of planning by the offender.

Intimate-partner assault: A gender-neutral term used to characterize assaultive behavior that takes place between individuals involved in an intimate relationship.

Mass murder: The illegal killing of four or more victims at one location within one event.

National Violence Against Women (NVAW) Survey: A national survey of the extent and nature of violence against women conducted between November 1995 and May 1996 and funded through grants from the National Institute of Justice and the U.S. Department of Health and Human Services' National Center for Injury Prevention and Control.

Nonprimary homicide: Murder that involves victims and offenders who have no prior relationship and that usually occurs during the course of another crime, such as robbery.

Personal robbery: Robbery that occurs on the highway or street or in a public place (and that is often referred to as "mugging") and robbery that occurs in residences.

Primary homicide: Murder involving family members, friends, and acquaintances.

Rape myth: A false assumption about rape, such as, "When a woman says no, she really means yes." Rape myths characterize much of the discourse surrounding sexual violence.

Rape shield law: A statute providing for the protection of rape victims by ensuring that defendants do not introduce irrelevant facts about the victim's sexual history into evidence.

Selective disinhibition: A loss of self-control due to the characteristics of the social setting, drugs or alcohol, or a combination of both.

Separation assault: Violence inflicted by partners on significant others who attempt to leave an intimate relationship.

Serial murder: Criminal homicide that involves the killing of several victims in three or more separate events.

Sibling offense: An offense or incident that culminates in homicide. The offense or incident may be a crime, such as robbery, or an incident that meets a less stringent criminal definition, such as a lover's quarrel involving assault or battery.

Spousal rape: The rape of one spouse by the other. The term usually refers to the rape of a woman by her husband.

Stalking: A course of conduct directed at a specific person that involves repeated visual or physical proximity; nonconsensual communication; verbal, written, or implied threats; or a combination thereof, which would cause a reasonable person fear. Also, a constellation of behaviors involving repeated attempts to impose on another person unwanted communication and/or contact.

Victim precipitation: Contributions made by the victim to the criminal event, especially those that led to its initiation.

Violence Against Women Act (VAWA):   A federal law enacted as a component of the 1994 Violent Crime Control and Law Enforcement Act and intended to address concerns about violence against women. The law focused on improving the interstate enforcement of protection orders, providing effective training for court personnel involved with women's issues, improving the training and collaboration of police and prosecutors with victim service providers, strengthening law enforcement efforts to reduce violence against women, and on increasing services to victims of violence. President Clinton signed the reauthorization of this legislation, known as the Violence Against Women Act 2000, into law on October 28, 2000.

Violent Criminal Apprehension Program (VICAP):   The program of the Federal Bureau of Investigation focusing on serial murder investigation and the apprehension of serial killers.

Workplace violence: The crimes of murder, rape, robbery, and assault committed against persons who are at work or on duty.

Questions for Review

1. What is a typology? What are some of the typologies of violent crime that this chapter discusses?
2. What are the key issues to be considered in explaining patterns of homicide?
3. What are the key issues to be considered in explaining as well as preventing the crimes of rape and child sexual abuse?
4. What are the different kinds of robbery that this chapter discusses? Describe the criminal careers of robbers.
5. What different kinds of assault can be identified? Describe what is known about intimate-partner violence.
6. Provide a useful definition of *workplace violence*. What do we know about the offense?
7. Explain the major patterns of stalking.

Questions for Reflection

1. Why are crime typologies useful for understanding patterns of violent crime?
2. Are violent crimes primarily rational activities?
3. Why was rape law reform necessary? What have been the beneficial aspects of reform for rape victims?
4. Is robbery primarily a rational activity? Why or why not?

Student Exercises

Activity #1

Recent legislation requires that universities publish statistics on crime on campus. Obtain information about violent crime occurring at your university campus. Compare the rates of serious violent crimes on campus to the rates in neighboring jurisdictions. How safe does your university appear to be?

Activity #2

Locate programs and other resources that are available on your university campus for victims of domestic violence and/or stalking. Bring these materials into class for discussion.

Activity #3

Obtain NCVS and UCR data on murder and aggravated assault and compare and contrast the two crimes. What are the similarities, and what are the differences between them? Consider factors such as the characteristics of the offenders and the victims, characteristics of the event (location, weapon used, when the crime occurred, etc.), and arrest and clearance rates.

Activity #4

Select three theories that you have discussed in previous chapters and discuss how each of these might explain the crimes of assault and robbery.

Criminology Today on the Web

www.icpsr.umich.edu/HRWG

This is the home page of the Homicide Research Working Group, which was organized by the American Society of Criminology in 1991.

www.pbs.org/kued/nosafeplace

This Web site provides a link to a 1998 PBS program discussing violence against women. The site includes the program script, links, and other resources.

www.cavnet2.org

This is the home page of CAVNET, the Communities Against Violence Network, which addresses domestic violence, sexual assault, rape, stalking, and other types of violent crime.

www.ncjrs.gov/pdffiles1/nij/210346.pdf

This is a PDF file presenting results from the 2006 National Violence Against Women Survey, which asked respondents about their experiences as victims of various types of intimate-partner violence, including rape, assault, and stalking.

www.ojp.usdoj.gov/ovw

This is the home page of the U.S. Department of Justice Violence Against Women Office.

www.usdoj.gov/criminal/cybercrime/cyberstalking.htm

This site makes available the 1999 Attorney General's report on cyberstalking.

www.antistalking.com

This is the home page of The Antistalking Web Site.

Student Study Guide Questions

True/False

_____ 1. Wolfgang found that the majority of homicides involved family members.

_____ 2. Men are more likely than women to be offenders and victims of homicides involving family members.

_____ 3. A homicide that occurs during an incident that began as a robbery is an example of an instrumental homicide.

_____ 4. Gang-affiliated violence involves violence as a direct result of gang activity.

_____ 5. Serial killers generally use a standard pattern of offending and method of killing.

_____ 6. Most serial killers are psychotic.

_____ 7. According to Kelleher and Kelleher, the black widow kills individuals in her care.

_____ 8. A predisposer is a long-term stable precondition that is incorporated into the mass murderer's personality.

_____ 9. The NCVS suggests that there are significantly more rapes in the United States than are reported in the UCR.

_____ 10. A rape myth is a true assumption about rape.

_____ 11. Prison rape only occurs in male institutions.

_____ 12. Feminist perspectives view gender as a biological given.

_____ 13. Sadistic rapes frequently involve torture.

_____ 14. Supremacy rapists are more interested in the punishment given to the victim than to the sexual contact, according to Dennis Stevens.

_____ 15. According to Diana Scully, rape is a socially learned behavior.

_____ 16. Institutional robberies may be prevented by environmental changes.

_____ 17. Firearms are less likely to be used during family assaults than in other aggravated assaults.

_____ 18. Men and women are equally likely to be victims of stalking.

Fill in the Blank

19. Gottfredson and Hirschi's general theory of crime is an example of a(n) _____ typology.

20. _____ homicides are generally motivated by interpersonal hostility.

21. Victim _____ focuses on characteristics of victims that may have led to their victimization.

22. Serial murder involves killing several victims in at least _____ separate events.

23. A comfort serial killer is motivated by _____.

24. According to Fox and Levin, _____ killers tend to be genuinely psychotic.

25. According to FBI profiling theory, _____ killers have higher levels of intelligence and social skills.

26. According to Levin and Fox, a _____ is a situation condition that increases the likelihood of a violent outburst.

27. _____ laws protect rape victims by ensuring that defendants do not introduce irrelevant facts of the victim's sexual past into evidence.

28. Rape of inmates by inmates is more common in _____ correctional institutions.

29. According to Groth, _____ rapists generally plan their crimes.

30. According to Baron and Straus, _____ refers to the inability of communities to sustain viable social institutions that serve as a buffer for social ills, such as crime.

31. According to Hazelwood and Burgess, the most common type of stranger rapist is the _____ rapist.

32. Dennis Stevens's typology of rapists suggests that _____ rapists hold friendship responsible for the rape.

33. Scully labeled rapists who claim that the sexual relations with the victims were consensual as _____.

34. Among homicides occurring during the commission of another felony, _____ is the most likely felony to result in a homicide.

35. _____ is the most frequently occurring violent crime.

36. _____ involves the use of electronic communication to harass individuals.

Multiple Choice

37. African Americans are disproportionately represented in the homicide statistics as
    a. victims.
    b. offenders.
    c. both victims and offenders.
    d. neither victims nor offenders.

38. Homicides that involve victims and offenders who have no prior relationship are classified as
    a. primary homicides.
    b. expressive crimes.
    c. nonprimary homicides.
    d. none of the above.

39. According to Williams and Flewelling, _____ is a stronger predictor of family homicide than of stranger homicide.

    a. poverty
    b. population size
    c. the context of the event
    d. the victim-offender relationship

40. _____ focuses on explaining the role that alcohol plays in homicide.

    a. The general theory of crime
    b. The subculture of violence thesis
    c. Selective disinhibition theory
    d. The critical criminological perspective

41. According to Fox and Levin, the _____ serial killer frequently plays a "cat and mouse" game with the victim before committing the murder.

    a. visionary
    b. comfort
    c. hedonistic
    d. power seeker

42. Which of the following is a type of mission-oriented serial killer?

    a. The dominance killer
    b. The profit-driven killer
    c. The reformist
    d. The sexual sadist

43. According to Levin and Fox's typology of mass murder, the most common motive for such a crime is

    a. revenge.
    b. love.
    c. profit.
    d. terror.

44. Which of the following was *not* required by the rules of evidence under the common-law definition of *rape*?

    a. The victim had to demonstrate physical resistance to the act.
    b. The victim must have some form of corroboration that the rape occurred.
    c. The victim's previous sexual history could be admitted as relevant information.
    d. The victim had to be the spouse of the offender.

45. Which of the following is *not* one of the types of rape identified in Groth's typology of rapists?

    a. Power rape
    b. Anger rape
    c. Sadistic rape
    d. Erotic rape

46. According to the Hazelwood and Burgess typology of rapists, _____ rapists plan their crimes and use a lot of force to subdue the victim.

    a. anger-excitation
    b. power-reassurance
    c. anger-retaliatory
    d. power-assertive

47. According to Hazelwood and Burgess, _____ rapists generally stalk their victims in advance and generally act out of a sense of social and sexual inadequacy.

    a. anger-retaliatory
    b. anger-excitation
    c. power-reassurance
    d. power-assertive

48. According to the Hazelwood and Burgess typology of rapists, the blitz approach is used by the _____ category of rapist.

    a. anger-excitation
    b. power-reassurance
    c. anger-retaliatory
    d. power-assertive

49. According to Dennis Stevens, the _____ rape motive involves an offender who believes that the victim is responsible for the attack because she consented to the sex in some "silent deal."

    a. lust
    b. righteous
    c. peer
    d. supremacy

50. Robbers who target drug dealers they do not know are employing the technique of

    a. anonymity maintenance.
    b. intimidation.
    c. hypervigilance.
    d. selective disinhibition.

51. Which of the following is *not* typical of an aggravated assault offender?

    a. Lower socioeconomic status
    b. Prior arrest record
    c. African American male
    d. Evidence of offense specialization

52. The most common workplace violent incident is a(n)

    a. robbery.
    b. homicide.
    c. assault.
    d. rape.

53. The first antistalking statute was passed in
    a. New York.
    b. California.
    c. Washington, D.C.
    d. Texas.

54. Stalking behaviors include
    a. following the victim.
    b. making phone calls.
    c. vandalizing property.
    d. all of the above

Word Search Puzzle

```
Y  S  S  N  H  A  V  R  M  C  C  U  O  T  N  S  L  L  M  G  A  N  O  T  U
Z  V  I  B  O  N  N  X  H  Z  K  E  K  W  F  P  K  Q  X  G  U  L  R  S  Q
L  U  E  F  M  Y  Z  Y  J  T  N  M  M  A  S  J  R  A  N  J  B  W  S  P  M
T  D  X  C  I  V  H  S  Z  F  C  J  P  W  G  Q  A  S  S  A  U  L  T  U  G
I  I  P  E  C  A  Z  L  I  O  H  I  N  S  T  R  U  M  E  N  T  A  L  C  P
Z  S  R  O  I  W  Z  I  T  U  I  R  R  V  C  A  J  R  P  B  Q  Y  S  Z  X
J  I  E  C  D  A  M  E  U  Z  B  I  M  Q  L  O  C  W  G  J  E  X  N  H  Z
P  N  S  O  E  Z  G  R  B  M  C  B  M  C  Q  D  A  U  Y  T  R  Z  B  R  H
O  H  S  V  R  L  D  N  G  J  S  D  E  M  J  N  O  N  P  R  I  M  A  R  Y
Y  I  I  P  V  C  S  U  R  O  B  B  E  R  Y  G  T  E  Z  M  L  V  O  I  I
M  B  V  X  O  I  F  J  I  X  T  H  C  Y  B  E  R  S  T  A  L  K  I  N  G
Y  I  E  P  W  H  A  B  K  T  A  H  O  M  H  F  A  O  Y  Y  L  J  R  H  S
B  T  E  E  F  K  A  C  Q  U  A  I  N  T  A  N  C  E  C  E  Q  K  I  V  A
B  I  Z  Q  X  A  B  D  B  I  I  C  D  O  S  U  U  A  P  Y  X  A  S  R  A
A  O  K  S  V  D  O  U  F  I  V  S  B  M  D  D  H  N  F  Q  K  B  Q  A  E
J  N  R  O  I  P  L  P  P  I  A  W  F  V  X  Y  V  S  Q  C  M  I  N  P  D
C  M  M  A  Y  V  C  H  C  R  J  C  L  E  Z  N  I  I  E  V  N  R  M  E  N
A  P  K  X  X  F  T  S  U  H  X  W  M  R  D  K  C  J  D  M  I  L  I  M  T
N  K  J  W  O  R  K  P  L  A  C  E  Z  V  M  A  A  V  U  N  Z  H  L  Y  Y
R  A  M  V  V  T  Q  Z  A  K  J  D  I  B  J  V  P  Q  S  V  P  W  N  T  P
V  R  H  Z  F  O  A  R  B  Y  S  R  L  K  I  U  E  M  G  F  L  W  H  H  O
B  N  R  L  J  A  T  S  N  D  U  O  X  R  O  Q  P  A  N  T  Z  R  U  S  L
T  P  R  X  S  P  T  N  I  F  M  T  E  S  A  S  T  A  L  K  I  N  G  R  O
K  N  L  N  C  P  R  E  C  I  P  I  T  A  T  I  O  N  G  K  K  D  Z  O  G
N  P  C  D  G  D  F  Z  Z  O  I  A  Z  N  I  C  L  N  G  F  F  U  N  Y  Y
```

Acquaintance	Assault	Cyberstalking	Disinhibition	Expressive	Homicide
Instrumental	Nonprimary	Precipitation	Rape myths	Robbery	Stalking
Typology	VAWA	VICAP	Workplace		

Crossword Puzzle

Across

1. Classification of crimes along a particular dimension, such as legal categories.
4. Repeated behaviors directed at a specific person that would cause a reasonable person fear.
6. A(n) _____ homicide involves victims and offenders who have no prior relationship.
7. A goal-directed crime that involves some degree of planning by the offender.
9. A(n) _____ murder involves the killing of several victims in three or more separate events.
10. The robbery of a gas station is an example of _____ robbery.
11. A(n) _____ offense is a crime that culminates in a homicide.
12. The victim's contributions to the criminal event.
13. Politically motivated violence against noncombatant targets by subnational groups or clandestine agents.
14. Mugging is an example of _____ robbery.
15. A crime resulting from acts of interpersonal hostility.

Down

2. A(n) _____ homicide involves family members, friends, and acquaintances.
3. _____ rape generally involves the rape of a woman by her husband.
5. Activities using the Internet or e-mail to harass a victim.
8. _____ rape involves a prior social relationship between the victim and the offender.

1 Crimes against Property

Learning Outcomes

After reading this chapter, students should be able to:

- Identify the major forms of property crime and explain the distinction between professional criminals and other kinds of property offenders
- Describe the prevalence of and list the types of larceny-theft
- Describe the prevalence of burglary and list the types of burglars and their motivations
- Explain the activities of stolen property receivers and describe how stolen goods are distributed
- Define *arson* and describe the activities of fire setters

Chapter Outline

Chapter Summary

This chapter discusses various types of property crime in the United States, including larceny-theft, burglary, stolen property, and arson. The difference between persistent thieves and professional criminals is examined briefly. Professional offenders commit crime with some skill, make a living from crime, and spend relatively little time incarcerated. Persistent thieves are those who continue in common-law property crimes despite having at best an ordinary level of success. Most property offenders do not specialize in one type of crime. The issue of property crimes as rational choice is also discussed.

Larceny-theft, which does not involve the use of force or illegal entry, is the most frequently occurring property crime, with theft from a motor vehicle being the largest category. Theft on college campuses is influenced by the size and design of the campus. Motor vehicle theft can include a variety of means of transportation, but automobiles are the vehicle most commonly stolen. It is the crime where the largest percentage of victims miss time from work as a result of the crime. Most completed motor vehicle thefts are reported to the police. Theft of external car parts may be committed for a variety of reasons; theft from motor vehicles also includes taking items from within the vehicle (stereo equipment, cameras, briefcases, etc.). Joyriding involves opportunistic car theft committed by groups of teenagers for fun or thrills; the preferred vehicle is an American-made sports car. Jockeys are professional car thieves who are regularly involved in steal-to-order jobs; they are rarer but represent the most costly and serious form of auto theft.

Employee theft and shoplifting are both increasing. Employee theft costs retailers more than customer shoplifting and is often perceived as more serious. Historically, shoplifting was pervasive among middle-class women. Today, it is a crime that crosses class lines and is not committed primarily by women; juveniles are overrepresented in current statistics on offending. Research suggests that shoplifting is one of the largest categories of unofficial delinquency and may be a gateway offense leading to more serious and chronic types of offending. Various typologies of shoplifters are discussed.

Burglary is usually a victim-avoiding crime; offenders prefer to avoid direct confrontation with their victims. Burglary is more common in large metropolitan areas and in the Midwest. Changes in routine activities since World War II may help explain changes in burglary rates. A typology of burglars is discussed. The primary motivation for burglary is the need for fast cash, often to maintain the offender's street status or to support a party lifestyle. Commercial targets are selected based on their suitability, with retail establishments being the most common choice. Residential burglars rarely target homes of family or friends but may target homes of people otherwise known to them. Other key elements in target selection include a reluctance to burglarize occupied dwellings, residences with complex security devices, and residences with a dog that could make noise or injure the offender. The recent increase in robbery and decrease in burglary may be linked to the increased demand for crack cocaine. Some burglaries have sexual motivations, such as voyeuristic or fetish burglaries; there may also be a link between burglary and later sexual offending.

Receiving stolen property involves three key elements: buying and selling, stolen property, and knowing property to be stolen. The fence is a middleman who takes on the role of moving stolen goods from the professional thief to the customer; most thieves do not use a professional fence to dispose of stolen goods. Paul Cromwell's typology of criminal receivers is discussed.

The FBI records an incident as arson only after it has been investigated and officially classified as arson by the proper investigative authorities; fires of suspicious or unknown origin are not included in the FBI's arson statistics. The recent wave of church arsons in the United States and the motivations behind these crimes are discussed. Arson for profit is fairly rare. The majority of those involved in arson are juveniles.

Key Concepts

Booster: A frequent shoplifter.

Fence: An individual or a group involved in the buying, selling, and distribution of stolen goods. Also called *criminal receiver*.

Gateway offense: An offense, usually fairly minor in nature, that leads to more serious offenses. Shoplifting, for example, may be a gateway offense to more serious property crimes.

Jockey: A professional car thief involved regularly in calculated, steal-to-order car thefts.

Joyriding: An opportunistic car theft, often committed by a teenager seeking fun or thrills.

Occasional offender: A criminal offender whose offending patterns are guided primarily by opportunity.

Offense specialization: A preference for engaging in a certain type of offense to the exclusion of others.

Persistent thief: One who continues in common-law property crimes despite no better than an ordinary level of success.

Professional criminal: A criminal offender who makes a living from criminal pursuits, is recognized by other offenders as professional, and engages in offending that is planned and calculated.

Snitch: An amateur shoplifter.

Questions for Review

1. What are the major forms of property crime that this chapter discusses? Explain the differences between professional property offenders and persistent property offenders.
2. What are the different kinds of larceny-theft discussed in this chapter, and how common is each?
3. How frequently does burglary occur? What are the types of burglars discussed in this chapter? How do the motivations of the various types of burglars differ? In what ways are they the same?
4. What kinds of illegal activities are receivers of stolen property generally involved in? How do stolen goods get resold?
5. What is arson and what different kinds of arson can be identified? What motivates arson?

Questions for Reflection

1. To what extent is "thrill seeking" a motivation behind certain types of property offenses? How might it contribute to the crime of shoplifting?
2. Why is so much attention given to shoplifting among adolescents? Should it be? Why or why not?
3. How are "honest" citizens and professional criminal receivers connected?
4. To what extent are property offenders rational actors? Use examples from larceny, burglary, and receipt of stolen property to illustrate your answer.

5. What does the "sexualized context" of burglary mean? How can burglary have a sexual component or motivation?

6. How are drugs involved in the offending patterns of some burglars? Might effective drug-treatment programs reduce the number of burglaries committed? Why?

Student Exercises

Activity #1

Recent legislation requires that universities publish statistics on crime on campus. Obtain information about property crime occurring at your university campus. Compare the rates of property crime on campus to the rates in neighboring jurisdictions. How safe does your university appear to be?

Activity #2

Your instructor will place you in groups and assign each group to a building on campus (for example, the university library, the student union, a dormitory). Examine this building and its occupants for vulnerability to property crime (burglary, theft, etc.). Develop at least three workable techniques for reducing the likelihood of property crime victimization for the occupants of this building.

Criminology Today on the Web

www.ojp.usdoj.gov/bjs/cvict.htm

This site provides summary findings from the National Crime Victimization Survey. Click on the property crime chart for more information about property crime trends in the United States.

www.ojp.usdoj.gov/bjs/glance/mvt.htm

This link provides information from the Bureau of Justice Statistics on the rates of motor vehicle theft in the United States.

www.fbi.gov/hq/cid/arttheft/arttheft.htm

This is a link to the Web site for the FBI's Art Theft Program.

www.bayou.com/~captjim/cheklist.html

The Rushton Police Department and the National Sheriff's Association have developed a home burglary prevention checklist to allow individuals to make security surveys of their own homes.

www.atf.treas.gov

This is the home page of the Bureau of Alcohol, Tobacco, Firearms and Explosives, which is the agency responsible for the investigation of arson of federal buildings.

www.usfa.dhs.gov/fireservice/subjects/fireprev/index.shtm

The U.S. Fire Administration's fire prevention page.

Student Study Guide Questions

True/False

_____ 1. Occasional offenders are so named because of the infrequency of their offenses.

_____ 2. The largest percentage of stolen vehicles are taken from a parking lot or garage.

_____ 3. Police are less able to identify stolen car parts than stolen vehicles.

_____ 4. Cars stolen by jockeys are likely to be recovered by the police.

_____ 5. Employee theft is a more serious problem than shoplifting to retailers.

_____ 6. Today, shoplifting is committed primarily by women.

_____ 7. Winona Ryder is not a typical shoplifter.

_____ 8. The least common type of shoplifter is the occasional, according to Richard Moore.

_____ 9. The majority of burglars are professionals.

_____ 10. Residential burglaries are more likely to occur during the morning hours.

_____ 11. According to Mike Maguire, middle-range burglars are more likely to be juveniles.

_____ 12. The pattern of victim-offender relationship found in property crimes is different from that found in violent crimes.

_____ 13. Most household burglaries involve economic loss.

_____ 14. Property crimes may have more of an effect than violent crimes on a victim's decision to move.

_____ 15. The use of a professional fence is the most common method of disposing of stolen goods for most thieves.

_____ 16. As a front for criminal activity, a pawnshop would be viewed as strictly clean.

_____ 17. Fires that are of suspicious or unknown origin are classified by the FBI as arson.

_____ 18. For juveniles between the ages of 8 and 12, fire setting generally represents underlying psychosocial conflicts.

Fill in the Blank

19. A(n) _____ thief continues in common law property crimes despite having an ordinary level of success, at best.

20. According to Alfred Blumstein, the _____ period is the initial phase of a property offender's criminal career.

21. _____ is the most frequently occurring property offense.

22. Removing air bags, radios, seats, and other parts from a stolen car is known as _____.

23. Joyriding offenses are usually committed by _____.

24. The most common reason why Finnish adolescents desist from shoplifting is _____.

25. According to Richard Moore's typology of shoplifters, _____ shoplifters are inexperienced, rarely plan the crime in advance, and are remorseful when apprehended.

26. According to Richard Moore, the _____ shoplifter is most likely to steal merchandise for resale to others.

27. According to McShane and Noonan's typology of shoplifters, members of the _____ group were characterized by a lack of apparent psychosocial stressors preceding apprehension.

28. According to victimization data, approximately _____% of households in the United States will be burglarized at least once over an average lifetime.

29. According to Mike Maguire's typology of burglars, _____ burglars are professionals.

30. Commercial burglary locations are usually selected based on the _____ of the target.

31. Retail establishments are _____ times as likely to be burglarized as other commercial establishments.

32. Crack users are more likely to commit _____ than burglary.

33. _____ burglaries occur when the offender steals particular items because they provide an outlet for sexual gratification.

34. A professional fence who deals in only certain types of stolen goods is known as a(n) _____.

35. A(n) _____ fence is one whose illicit lines of goods are distinct from those of legitimate commerce.

36. The Church Arson Prevention Act was signed into law by President Clinton in _____.

Multiple Choice

37. Malcolm Kline used the term _____ to refer to the heterogeneous and un-planned nature of offending found among gang members.
    a. professional criminal activity
    b. offense specialization
    c. cafeteria-style offending
    d. persistent offending

38. According to Alfred Blumstein, the break-in period of a property offender's criminal career lasts approximately _____ years.

    a. 5
    b. 10
    c. 20
    d. 25

39. The most common index crime occurring on college campuses is

    a. larceny.
    b. burglary.
    c. assault.
    d. rape.

40. The primary motivation for the crime of joyriding is

    a. profit.
    b. fun.
    c. to meet a long-term need for transportation.
    d. to meet an immediate need for transportation.

41. Shoplifting is

    a. increasing.
    b. decreasing.
    c. remaining the same.
    d. Research has not addressed this.

42. One of the best ways to address both shoplifting and employee theft is

    a. security personnel.
    b. technology.
    c. severe penalties.
    d. warning notices.

43. Today, _____ are overrepresented in offense statistics on shoplifting.

    a. juveniles
    b. young adults
    c. senior citizens
    d. middle-class women

44. Research by _____ suggests that males are more likely to shoplift than females.

    a. Mary Owen Cameron
    b. Lloyd W. Klemke
    c. Richard H. Moore
    d. Frank J. McShane and Barrie A. Noonan

45. According to Mary Owen Cameron's typology, professional shoplifters were known as

    a. boosters.
    b. impulsive shoplifters.
    c. snitches.
    d. enigmas.

46. According to Mary Owen Cameron's typology, shoplifters who primarily stole for their own personal gratification were known as
    a. boosters.
    b. impulsive shoplifters.
    c. snitches.
    d. enigmas.

47. According to Richard Moore's typology of shoplifters, _____ shoplifters generally had psychological problems.
    a. impulsive
    b. episodic
    c. amateur
    d. occasional

48. According to McShane and Noonan's typology of shoplifters, the _____ category includes persons who are older, with higher levels of education than other groups, and more likely to be married and male.
    a. rebel
    b. enigma
    c. reactionary
    d. infirm

49. According to UCR data, the most common type of burglary involves _____ entry.
    a. forcible
    b. attempted forcible
    c. unlawful
    d. lawful

50. According to Mike Maguire's typology of burglars, juveniles committing crimes on the spur of the moment fall into the category of _____ burglars.
    a. high-level
    b. mid-range
    c. low-level
    d. multilevel

51. Which of the following is *not* one of the ways residential burglars generally select targets?
    a. Through their knowledge of the occupants
    b. Through spur of the moment selection
    c. Through receiving a tip
    d. Through observing a potential target

52. _____ conducted a case study of Sam Goodman, a professional fence.
    a. Carl Klockars
    b. Darrell Steffensmeier
    c. Vincent Swaggi
    d. Paul Cromwell

53. According to Cromwell's typology of criminal receivers, _____ receivers generally buy stolen property primarily for personal consumption.
    a. professional
    b. avocational
    c. amateur
    d. episodic

54. Young children under the age of seven generally start fires
    a. accidentally.
    b. due to underlying psychosocial conflicts.
    c. for revenge.
    d. for personal motives.

Word Search Puzzle

```
H J N I H O K U D D S C F W X O E F K H F K O R P
X B T R S D G C G U T K C R B G Q A W Y U R B C M
K O L Q Q L Q W K O W S A D S A L A G U P D T W A
D U K B J X P T D X W D R R N T J L H T E V M X I
J Y I L F B B X M A L Y D A U E H Y Z N R X Q W I
G T S M G Y B L B R F E N C E W A W T W S T X E T
L O J U P C A T Q N E S A X A A X E F A I K M O G
P N Y T J B N B Q S K Q P D G Y N L N F S X F C M
E Z D I Q T V W L O W M A C E Z M X W Y T T B F P
S H P C Q N C N Z C M P I U R B O O S T E R S C E
A A U C Z Z W J J F J N P L B E F K J J N S T X L
E U S P E C I A L I Z A T I O N G U E Q T N T C K
W M C M V T Q O T P K G S W L K R V P L O I Q A Q
M Y P V C I N G J N B J S J N Y W M P K S T B O A
Q V K L Z F A D K C L O T D X V X I E F V C N H I
I B M A X S V Y Y S Q C W Z A P L R X E N H P P B
G L L N M Q G Z N H N K F M X M W N A H V J Z T B
L R V A D Y M L Q U V E K F A J X P G G H E V O Y
W J X C X V G B X Z J Y G K O C C A S I O N A L L
U Z B E K J W V Z Y S V P X C Z H S L M V J F Y J
N Q U M J Z W L W A Y Y T F H W D O D V U I N A R
G U Q V Q T O N I X Q Z A Q A Y Q O R M Q J Y F C
N P X E V W B R Z H P B M J O Y R I D I N G B V L
D E A F P R O F E S S I O N A L C P W A Y G S V Y
B S M S J U O M H Z F M C S D J G Y Z M F O W A W
```

Booster   Fence   Gateway   Jockey   Joyriding   Occasional
Persistent   Professional   Snitch   Specialization

Crossword Puzzle

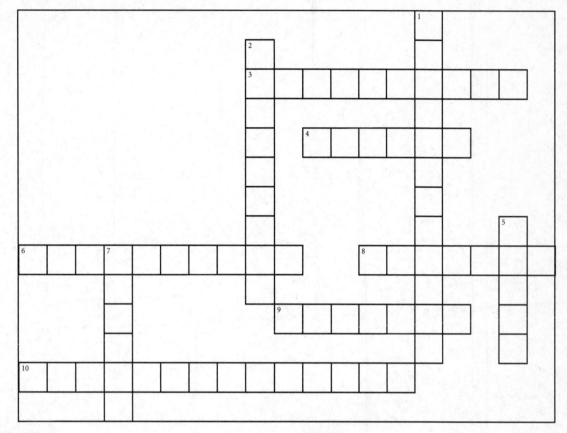

Across

3. An offender whose offending patterns are guided primarily by opportunity.
4. A professional car thief involved in steal-to-order car thefts.
6. A(n) _____ thief continues committing property crimes despite no better than an ordinary level of success.
8. A frequent shoplifter.
9. Shoplifting may be a(n) _____ offense to more serious crime.
10. A preference for committing a certain type of crime.

Down

1. A criminal who makes a living from crime.
2. An opportunistic car theft, often committed by a teenager seeking fun or thrills.
5. An individual involved in the buying, selling, and distribution of stolen goods.
7. An amateur shoplifter.

12

White-Collar and Organized Crime

Learning Outcomes

After reading this chapter, students should be able to:

- Meaningfully discuss white-collar crime and its conceptualization
- Describe the nature of organized crime and be able to list some significant organized criminal groups operating today
- Recommend some policies for the control of organized crime

Chapter Outline

Chapter Summary

This chapter reviews two specific categories of crime: white-collar crime and organized crime. Edwin Sutherland's original 1939 definition of *white-collar crime* focused on the social standing of the offender; today, the focus has shifted to the type of offense committed. Currently, one commonly used term is *occupational crime*, which includes any criminal act committed through opportunities created in the course of a legal occupation. Gary S. Green developed a typology of occupational crime that includes four categories: organizational occupational crime, state authority occupational crime, professional occupational crime, and individual occupational crime. Corporate crime, another form of white-collar crime, is committed for the benefit of the corporation rather than the individual employee. One new area of corporate crime is environmental crime. There have been a number of attempts to explain white-collar crime. Sutherland applied elements of differential association theory to white-collar crime. Travis Hirschi and Michael Gottfredson stated that white-collar criminals are motivated by the same forces that drive other offenders and suggest that a general theory of crime can explain white-collar crime and other forms of crime as well. John Braithwaite states that white-collar criminals are motivated by a disparity between corporate goals and legitimate means and suggests that business subcultures encourage illegal behavior. Dealing with white-collar crime may require ethical, enforcement, structural, and political reforms.

Criminal societies such as La Cosa Nostra and the Mafia began in Italy several centuries ago and migrated to the United States during a period of Italian immigration during the late 1800s. Prohibition, which began after the passage of the Eighteenth Amendment to the U.S. Constitution in 1919, established the wealth and power of modern organized crime syndicates and effectively institutionalized official corruption. The Wickersham Commission specifically mentioned the corrupting influence that Prohibition was having on professional law enforcement in the United States. During this period, organized crime leaders also worked to consolidate power. The repeal of the Eighteenth Amendment, in 1933, ended Prohibition. Organized crime activities went underground for the next 20 years. National attention was again focused on organized crime in 1951, when the federal Kefauver Committee reported that a nationwide crime syndicate was operating in many large U.S. cities. Eventually, federal investigations established the existence of 24 crime families operating in the United States under the direction of a commission.

Organized crime activities include racketeering, vice, theft/fence rings, gangs, and terrorism. The primary motivation for all organized crime activities is money. Members of organized Sicilian American criminal groups are governed by a strict code of conduct known as *omertà*, which functions to concentrate power in the hands of the crime bosses as well as ensuring their protection. The two key requirements imposed by the code are to obey one's superiors and to keep silent; the penalty for failing to adhere to these rules is death. Transnational organized crime involves unlawful activity undertaken and supported by organized criminal groups operating across national boundaries; it is becoming a key challenge to law enforcement agencies. The most important piece of federal legislation ever passed to target organized crime activities is RICO, which includes a provision for asset forfeiture, making it possible for federal officials to seize all proceeds of persons involved in racketeering. Organized crime is difficult to control; the text discusses various approaches to the control of organized criminal activity.

Key Concepts

Asset forfeiture: The authorized seizure of money, negotiable instruments, securities, or other things of value. In federal antidrug laws, the authorization of judicial representatives to seize all monies, negotiable instruments, securities, or other things of value furnished or intended to be furnished by any person in exchange for a controlled substance, and all proceeds traceable to such an exchange.

Bank fraud: Fraud or embezzlement that occurs within or against financial institutions that are insured or regulated by the U.S. government. Financial institution fraud includes commercial loan fraud, check fraud, counterfeit negotiable instruments, mortgage fraud, check kiting, and false credit applications.

Corporate crime: A violation of a criminal statute either by a corporate entity or by its executives, employees, or agents acting on behalf of and for the benefit of the corporation, partnership, or other form of business entity.

La Cosa Nostra: Literally, "our thing." A criminal organization of Sicilian origin. Also called *the Mafia, the Outfit, the Mob, the syndicate*, or simply *the organization*.

Environmental crime: A violation of the criminal law that, although typically committed by businesses or by business officials, may also be committed by other people or by organizational entities and which damages some protected or otherwise significant aspect of the natural environment.

Ethnic succession: The continuing process whereby one immigrant or ethnic group succeeds another by assuming its position in society.

Insider trading: Equity trading based on confidential information about important events that may affect the price of the issue being traded.

Kefauver Committee: The popular name for the federal Special Committee to Investigate Originated Crime in Interstate Commerce, formed in 1951.

Mafia: See **La Cosa Nostra**.

Money laundering: The process of converting illegally earned assets, originating as cash, to one or more alternative forms to conceal such incriminating factors as illegal origin and true ownership.

Occupational crime: Any act punishable by law that is committed through opportunity created in the course of an occupation that is legal.

Omertà: The informal, unwritten code of organized crime, which demands silence and loyalty, among other things, of family members.

Organized crime: The unlawful activities of the members of a highly organized, disciplined association engaged in supplying illegal goods and services, including gambling, prostitution, loan-sharking, narcotics, and labor racketeering.

Racketeer Influenced and Corrupt Organizations (RICO): A statute that was part of the federal Organized Crime Control Act of 1970 and that is intended to combat criminal conspiracies.

Securities fraud: The theft of money resulting from intentional manipulation of the value of equities, including stocks and bonds. Securities fraud also includes theft from securities accounts and wire fraud.

Transnational organized crime: Unlawful activity undertaken and supported by organized criminal groups operating across national boundaries.

White-collar crime: Violations of the criminal law committed by persons of respectability and high social status in the course of their occupation.

Questions for Review

1. What is white-collar crime? How did the idea of white-collar crime develop in the criminological literature?
2. What is organized crime? How does it differ from white-collar crime?
3. What strategies does this chapter discuss for combating the activities of organized crime? Which seem best to you? Why? Can you think of any other strategies that might be effective? If so, what are they?

Questions for Reflection

1. What linkages, if any, might exist between white-collar and organized crime?
2. What types of white-collar crime has this chapter identified? Is corporate crime a form of white-collar crime? Is occupational crime a form of white-collar crime?
3. Describe a typical organized crime family, as outlined in this chapter. Why does a crime family contain so many different "levels"?
4. What is money laundering? How might money laundering be reduced or prevented? Can you think of any strategies this chapter does not discuss for the reduction of money laundering activities in the United States? If so, what are they?

Student Exercises

Activity #1

Explain how the routine activity approach to explaining crime might be applied to organized crime.

Activity #2

Obtain a chart showing the organizational structure of a modern legitimate corporation. Compare this to Figure 12.1, which shows the structure of a typical organized crime family. How do the structures differ? What similarities do you see?

Criminology Today on the Web

www.usdoj.gov/atr

This is the home page of the U.S. Department of Justice Antitrust Division, which is responsible for enforcing antitrust laws.

www.epa.gov

This is the home page for the U.S. Environmental Protection Agency.

www.occ.treas.gov/moneylaundering2002.pdf

This booklet provides information on money laundering and discusses ways that banks can protect themselves against becoming involved in money laundering schemes.

www.nw3c.org

This is the home page of the National White Collar Crime Center, which provides support services for law enforcement agencies that are involved in the prevention, investigation, and prosecution of economic and high-tech crimes.

www.wccfighter.com

This is the home page for *White-Collar Crime Fighter*, an online newsletter.

www4.law.cornell.edu/uscode/18/ch96.html

This site provides the full text of Title 18, Chapter 96 of the U.S. Code, the Racketeer Influenced and Corrupt Organizations Act (RICO).

Student Study Guide Questions

True/False

_____ 1. Sutherland found that white-collar criminals are more likely to be investigated than other types of offenders.

_____ 2. Blue-collar crime involves crimes committed by members of less prestigious occupational groups.

_____ 3. The Union Carbide Corporation liability case centered on the issue of criminal negligence.

_____ 4. Hirschi and Gottfredson have outlined a theory that is specific to white-collar crime.

_____ 5. John Braithwaite suggests that corporate officers are motivated to evade the law despite the generally positive relationship that exists between businesses and the government agencies that regulate them.

_____ 6. Most Sicilians who emigrated to the United States had ties to or experience with Mafia organizations in Italy.

_____ 7. According to the Wickersham Commission, Prohibition had a corrupting influence on police in America.

_____ 8. According to the Kefauver Committee, the American Mafia has international linkages that appear most clearly in connection with the narcotics trade.

_____ 9. Organized crime families may infiltrate legitimate businesses for the purpose of money laundering.

_____ 10. The code of omertà functions to ensure the protection of crime bosses.

_____ 11. One of the general features of the code of organized crime is to be a "stand-up" guy.

_____ 12. One hallmark of a true criminal organization is that it has a continuity over time as personnel within the organization change.

_____ 13. Many Russian private security firms are fronts for Russian gangsters and organized criminals.

_____ 14. RICO made racketeering illegal.

_____ 15. Asset forfeiture was authorized by the Hobbs Act.

_____ 16. The Bank of Credit and Commerce International was significantly involved in money laundering for drug cartels and terrorist organizations.

_____ 17. Federal statutes, such as the Money Laundering Control Act, have succeeded in reducing the problem of money laundering in the United States.

_____ 18. According to Gary Potter, to attack organized crime, society must meet the demands of the consumers of organized crime's products and services.

Fill in the Blank

19. According to Sutherland, white-collar crime involves crimes committed by a person of _____ social status.

20. The early definition of *white-collar crime* focused on the _____.

21. A crime committed by an attorney in his capacity as an attorney is an example of a(n) _____ occupational crime.

22. Braithwaite has recommended the implementation of a(n) _____ model as a way of reducing white-collar offending.

23. The 1914 _____ Act prohibited mergers and acquisitions in which the effect may be to create a monopoly.

24. The elimination of campaign contributions from businesses is an example of the _____ area of white-collar crime reform.

25. The Italian _____, based in Naples, was infamous for murder and extortion during the nineteenth century.

26. _____ refers to the continuing process by which one immigrant group supplants another through assumption of a particular place in society.

27. During Prohibition, organized crime leaders worked to _____ power.

28. In the case of _____, the convictions of Joseph Bonanno and 26 other well-known organized crime figures were overturned.

29. According to the President's Crime Commission, there are _____ groups operating as criminal cartels in large cities across the United States.

30. The function of the _____ within a crime family is to collect information for the boss.

31. The function of the _____ within a crime family are to serve as chiefs of operating units.

32. A total of _____ of the 24 crime families operate out of New York.

33. Al Capone's Chicago Organization currently operates in Chicago as the _____.

34. The majority of cocaine entering the United States illegally has been handled by _____ organized criminal groups.

35. The _____ Act made it a violation of federal law to engage in any criminal behavior that interferes with interstate commerce.

36. _____ is the process by which illegal gains are disguised as legal income.

Multiple Choice

37. White-collar crime was originally defined by
    a. Émile Durkheim.
    b. Edwin Sutherland.
    c. Richard Quinney.
    d. George Vold.

38. Currently, the concept of white-collar crime focuses on the
    a. nature of the crime.
    b. person involved.
    c. occupation involved.
    d. work environment.

39. According to Gary Green's typology of occupational crime, _____ occupational crimes benefit the employing agency.
    a. professional
    b. state authority
    c. organizational
    d. individual

40. Employee theft is an example of _____ occupational crime.
    a. organizational
    b. individual
    c. state authority
    d. professional

41. The fires set in Kuwait oil fields by retreating Iraqi Army troops during the 1991 Gulf War are an example of both ecological terrorism and _____ crime.
    a. occupational
    b. environmental
    c. state authority
    d. organizational occupational

42. Which of the following forces does *not* motivate white-collar criminals, according to Hirschi and Gottfredson?
    a. The avoidance of pain
    b. The pursuit of pleasure
    c. Self-interest
    d. Danger and excitement

43. According to Coleman, enforcement reforms include all but which of the following?
    a. Increasing the funding for enforcement agencies that deal with white-collar crime
    b. Increasing the level of fairness in determining government grants, purchases, and contracts
    c. Providing larger research budgets for regulatory investigators
    d. Insulating enforcement personnel from undue political influence

44. Changing the process by which corporations are chartered to include control over white-collar crime is an example of the _____ area of white-collar crime reform.
    a. ethical
    b. enforcement
    c. structural
    d. political

45. The key to the transformation of organized crime from "small time" to "big business" was
   - a. Prohibition.
   - b. prostitution.
   - c. gambling.
   - d. the Kefauver Commission report.

46. Which of the following was *not* one of the conclusions reached by the Kefauver Committee?
   - a. A nationwide crime syndicate exists with influence in many large cities.
   - b. The American Mafia has international linkages, especially in narcotics trafficking.
   - c. Mafia leaders usually control the most lucrative rackets in their cities.
   - d. Leadership appears to be centered in a single individual, rather than in a group.

47. The consigliere is also known as the
   - a. boss.
   - b. underboss.
   - c. counselor.
   - d. lieutenant.

48. The _____ are the lowest level of family membership.
   - a. soldiers
   - b. lieutenants
   - c. agents
   - d. consigliere

49. _____ involves the intimidation of legitimate businesses through threats of strikes, walkouts, and sabotage.
   - a. Labor union racketeering
   - b. Loan-sharking
   - c. Infiltration of legitimate businesses
   - d. None of the above

50. Unlawful activity undertaken and supported by organized criminal groups operating across national boundaries is known as _____ organized crime.
   - a. international
   - b. intercontinental
   - c. transnational
   - d. overseas

51. The _____ Act made it a crime to use the mail in support of activities such as gambling and loan-sharking.
   - a. RICO
   - b. Hobbs
   - c. BICI
   - d. Omertà

52. Which of the following would be an example of increasing the risk of involvement in organized crime?

    a. Putting more law enforcement officers on the streets
    b. Passing asset forfeiture statutes
    c. Creating educational programs and scholarships
    d. Legalizing gambling

53. Abadinsky's suggestion that a special good faith exception to the exclusionary rule in prosecutions involving RICO violations be provided falls under which of his approaches to controlling organized crime?

    a. Increasing the risk of involvement in organized crime
    b. Increasing law enforcement authority
    c. Reducing the economic lure of involvement
    d. Decreasing opportunity for organized criminal activity

54. Legalizing or decriminalizing illegal drugs falls into which of Abadinsky's approaches to controlling organized crime?

    a. Increasing the risk of involvement in organized crime
    b. Increasing law enforcement authority
    c. Reducing the economic lure of involvement
    d. Decreasing opportunity for organized criminal activity

Word Search Puzzle

```
S M X G D D F N Y Q V W V M R I C O T R X T P L N
A I R J A W V L T I B S H S G I N P J G E Q G A D
L Z K Z B C V W I F Z I O V Y F Y Q D C M Z G C M
J X O N Z L A S Y T X G H H L G V A F N F R G O W
P L C R A L F C W R E X F O R F E I T U R E N S P
L V Y I B X Y K D S H C K K F P C O X R Z Y A J
G C G X U M B W F L X R J J H Z K Y O C C O F N V
X T E R P T M O V O Z B U L N V D R R T Y Y R O Y
L D N X T O R G A N I Z E D S T M R X Q E U A S L
S N V M X Q P N X Y D I K N Q B Y O K E P B U T D
A M I A B S E Y J X J I S E F F K G F A D W D R A
G F R Q V X O C G L S M G O S V G B X P W F E A X
J I O Q R S U C C E S S I O N H R D Q Q L J V B D
A R N M O R C S G L M C O R P O R A T E M C Z W E
O N M Y M I E M R B A N I A W Q P T H D Y T Q K Z
B W E K E N H H Q A F J Z C T X A C Z W D I D N Z
H A N Y R I P H S E I T Q L E B O A H A S A T L M
P S T K T T A P H Z A D Z D S A V E T Y T R H S B
K S A W A R X F W I S Z V U H F K H A H K S R Q A
T E L N W O C C U P A T I O N A L B X Y X J J B N
G T B P K W J M T N K X T R A N S N A T I O N A L
V U E K E F A U V E R W C Q A R H F E K K W F P K
N E Z H P H W H I T E C O L L A R O G P S Z O H K
H A A N J C M E P T R N D Z T A F B I P Q K N O L
D I E N X V Y M H A H Z O K V W T A N J K E L N B
```

Asset	Corporate	Fraud	La cosa nostra	Environmental
Forfeiture	Kefauver	Mafia	Occupational	Omerta
Organized	RICO	Succession	Transnational	White collar

Crossword Puzzle

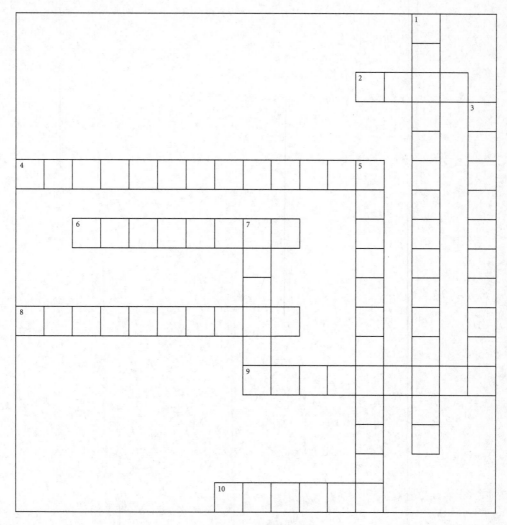

Across

2. A statute intended to combat criminal conspiracies.
4. _____ organized crime is committed by organized criminal groups operating across national boundaries.
6. The federal committee formed in 1951 to investigate organized crime.
8. Money _____ is the process of converting illegally earned cash into other forms to conceal incriminating factors.
9. A crime committed by employees acting on behalf of the company.
10. The informal, unwritten code of organized crime.

Down

1. The theft of money resulting from intentional manipulation of the value of equities (two words).
3. Asset _____ is the authorized seizure of money or other items of value.
5. A criminal organization of Sicilian origin (three words).
7. _____ succession is the process by which one immigrant group succeeds another.

13 Public Order and Drug Crimes

Learning Outcomes

After reading this chapter, students should be able to:

- Provide an overview of the history of drugs, drug abuse, and drug control legislation in the United States
- Define *dangerous drugs*, identify the types of psychoactive substances that are controlled by law, and describe their characteristics and effects
- Describe drug trafficking and government efforts to curtail it
- Explain the relationship between drug trafficking, drug use, and other forms of crime
- Identify the pros and cons of various drug-control strategies
- Define *prostitution* and describe various kinds of prostitutes and their clients

Chapter Outline

Introduction
History of Drug Abuse in the United States
    Extent of Abuse
    Young People and Drugs
    Costs of Abuse
Types of Illegal Drugs
    Stimulants
    Depressants
    Cannabis
    Narcotics
    Hallucinogens
    Anabolic Steroids
    Inhalants
    Pharmaceutical Diversion and Designer Drugs
Drug Trafficking
Drugs and Crime
    Illegal Drugs and Official Corruption
Social Policy and Drug Abuse
    Recent Legislation
    Drug-Control Strategies
    The National Drug-Control Policy
    Alternative Drug Policies

Prostitution

> *Morals Legislation*
> *A Typology of Prostitutes*
> *Clients of Prostitutes*
> *Feminist Perspectives on Prostitution*
> *Legalization and Decriminalization*

Chapter Summary

Drugs, and the relationship of drugs to crime, is one of the most significant policy issues today. There are a number of sources of data on drug abuse in the United States; this chapter reviews the findings of several recent surveys of both juveniles and adults. The costs of drug abuse are extremely difficult to measure, as they include not only measurable expenditures (law enforcement activities, criminal justice case processing, drug-treatment programs, etc.) but also related costs (illness and death resulting from exposure to controlled substances, drug-related crime, family fragmentation caused by illegal drug use, attitudinal change, etc.). There are seven main categories of controlled substances: stimulants, depressants, cannabis, narcotics, hallucinogens, anabolic steroids, and inhalants. In addition, there is a separate eighth category, dangerous drugs, which refers to broad categories or classes of controlled substances other than cocaine, opiates, and cannabis products.

Drug trafficking includes the manufacturing, distributing, dispensing, importing, and exporting of a controlled or counterfeit substance. Most cocaine comes into the United States from the Western Hemisphere, especially from South America; it is smuggled in primarily aboard maritime vessels. The Drug Enforcement Agency's heroin signature program tracks heroin trafficking and has found that the majority of heroin in the United States originates in South America.

Drug-defined crimes include violations of laws prohibiting or regulating the possession, use, or distribution of illegal drugs. Drug-related crimes are crimes in which drugs contribute to the offense. There is clear evidence of a strong relationship between drug use and crime. Drugs are also linked to official corruption; studies of police corruption have found that much illegal police activity was drug-related. Corrections officials may also be involved in drug-related corruption.

The text discusses the history of drug-control policy in the United States, beginning with the 1906 federal Pure Food and Drug Act, which required manufacturers to list their ingredients and specifically targeted mood-altering chemicals. The Comprehensive Drug Abuse Prevention and Control Act, passed in 1970, may be the most comprehensive piece of federal legislation to address controlled substances. The Violent Crime Control and Law Enforcement Act of 1994 also included a number of drug-related provisions. There are five main types of policy initiatives in the fight against illicit drugs. Current policy emphasizes antidrug legislation and strict enforcement. Interdiction is an international drug-control policy that focuses on stopping drugs from entering the country illegally. Crop control involves the eradication of drug crops, both in the United States and abroad. Asset forfeiture allows judicial representatives to seize any items that were involved in drug trafficking or sale. Antidrug education and drug treatment have become extremely popular recently. School-based programs such as D.A.R.E. have increased, although recent research has begun to question the effectiveness of D.A.R.E.-type interventions.

The Office of National Drug Control Policy was established in 1988, with the mission of establishing policies, priorities, and objectives for the national drug-control program. The goals of the program are to reduce illicit drug use, manufacturing, and trafficking; to reduce drug-related crime and violence; and to ameliorate drug-related health consequences.

The "war on drugs" has been extremely expensive. As a result of the "war on drugs," all phases of the criminal justice system have become drug-driven; the civil justice system has also been affected. Rates of imprisonment for drug offenders have increased significantly as a result of strict enforcement and a policy of incarceration.

Alternative drug-control policies are based on the assumption that drug abuse will never be eliminated. Decriminalization involves the reduction of criminal penalties associated with personal possession of a controlled substance. Legalization eliminates the laws and penalties that prohibit the production, sale, distribution, and possession of a controlled substance. There is a variety of arguments for and against legalization of drugs in the United States today.

Prostitution is defined as the offering of one's self for hire for the purpose of engaging in sexual relations, or the act or practice of engaging in sexual activity for money or its equivalent. Laws against prostitution relate to the issue of to what extent the law should legislate morality. The main types of prostitutes include streetwalkers, bar/hotel prostitutes, call girls, hotel/brothel prostitutes, and others who do not clearly fit any of these categories. A recent study of prostitutes' clients, or "johns," found that they ranged in age from 18 to 84 years, with a median age of 37, and were less likely to be married than other men. Almost three-quarters had attended some college. Approximately 20% demonstrated acceptance of at least four rape myths; this group may be responsible for perpetrating violent acts against women for hire.

Some feminist thinkers argue that prostitution exploits and demeans women, and subjects them to the dangers of violence and disease; they reject the idea that prostitution can be reformed. Others suggest that selling sex is not inherently exploitative and can be liberating because it fulfills a woman's rights to control her body and sexuality; this group sees prostitution as legitimate sex work and is more likely to argue for legalization. Legalization of prostitution would allow women above a specified age to offer paid sexual services with few restrictions. Decriminalization would reduce the penalties associated with prostitution but would regulate the practice and may attempt to curtail it. There are a variety of arguments for and against legalization of prostitution.

Key Concepts

Arrestee Drug Abuse Monitoring (ADAM) Program: A National Institute of Justice program that tracks trends in the prevalence and types of drug use among booked arrestees in urban areas.

Dangerous drug: A term used by the Drug Enforcement Administration to refer to "broad categories or classes of controlled substances other than cocaine, opiates, and cannabis products." Amphetamines, methamphetamines, PCP (phencyclidine), LSD, methcathinone, and "designer drugs" are all considered to be dangerous drugs.

Decriminalization: The redefinition of certain previously criminal behaviors into regulated activities that become "ticketable" rather than "arrestable."

Designer drugs: "New substances designed by slightly altering the chemical makeup of other illegal or tightly controlled drugs."

Drug-defined crime: A violation of the laws prohibiting or regulating the possession, use, or distribution of illegal drugs.

Drug-related crime: A crime in which drugs contribute to the offense (excluding violations of drug laws).

Drug trafficking: Manufacturing, distributing, dispensing, importing, and exporting (or possession with intent to do the same) a controlled substance or a counterfeit substance.

Heroin signature program (HSP): A Drug Enforcement Administration program that identifies the geographic source of a heroin sample through the detection of specific chemical characteristics in the sample peculiar to the source area.

Interdiction: An international drug-control policy that aims to stop drugs from entering the country illegally.

Legalization: Elimination of the laws and criminal penalties associated with certain behaviors—usually the production, sale, distribution, and possession of a controlled substance.

National Survey on Drug Use and Health (NSDUH): A national survey of illicit drug use among people 12 years of age and older that is conducted annually by the Substance Abuse and Mental Health Services Administration.

Office of National Drug Control Policy (ONDCP): A national office charged by Congress with establishing policies, priorities, and objectives for the nation's drug-control program. ONDCP is responsible for developing and disseminating the *National Drug-Control Strategy*.

Pharmaceutical diversion: The process by which legitimately manufactured controlled substances are diverted for illicit use.

Prostitution: The offering of one's self for hire for the purpose of engaging in sexual relations, or the act or practice of engaging in sexual activity for money or its equivalent.

Psychoactive substance: A substance that affects the mind, mental processes, or emotions.

Questions for Review

1. What are some of the laws that criminalize and restrict the use of drugs in the United States, and what drugs do they control? How did those laws come into being, and why?
2. What is a *dangerous drug*? What are the various controlled-substance categories described by federal law. How do the types of illegal drugs discussed in this chapter fit into those categories?
3. How do controlled substances reach the drug-consuming portion of the American public? How might drug trafficking be curtailed?
4. What is the relationship between drug trafficking, drug abuse, and other forms of crime?
5. What government efforts have been made to reduce the incidence of drug use in America? What are the pros and cons of each?
6. What is prostitution? What are the various types of prostitutes identified in this chapter?

Questions for Reflection

1. This book emphasizes a social problems versus social responsibility theme. Which of the social policy approaches to controlling drug abuse discussed in this chapter (if any) appear to be predicated upon a social problems approach? Which (if any) are predicated upon a social responsibility approach? Explain the nature of the relationship.

2. What are some of the costs of illicit drug use in the United States today? Which costs can be more easily reduced than others? How would you reduce the costs of illegal drug use?

3. What is the difference between decriminalization and legalization? Should drug use remain illegal? What do you think of the arguments in favor of legalization? Those against?

4. What is asset forfeiture? How has asset forfeiture been used in the fight against illegal drugs? How have recent U.S. Supreme Court decisions limited federal asset seizures? Do you agree that such limitations were necessary? Why?

5. How is prostitution like other crimes? How does it differ?

6. Do you think that prostitution should be legalized? Why or why not?

Student Exercises

Activity #1

Write a short paper discussing the advantages and disadvantages of legalizing marijuana in the United States. Include your personal opinion on the question of legalization and explain why you feel this way.

Activity #2

Write a short paper discussing the advantages and disadvantages of legalizing prostitution in the United States. Include your personal opinion on the question of legalization and explain why you feel this way.

Activity #3

Go to the Drug Enforcement Administration Web site (www.usdoj.gov/dea) and answer the following questions:

1. What is the "red ribbon campaign," and how did it begin?
2. What is the DEA's Mobile Enforcement Team?
3. Explain the DEA's Demand Reduction Program, including its goals and objectives
4. What was Operation Zorro II, and why was it unique?
5. What was the French Connection?
6. What is the mission of the DEA?

Criminology Today on the Web

www.usdoj.gov/dea
This is the home page of the Drug Enforcement Administration.

www.dare.com
This is the official Web site for D.A.R.E.

www.nida.nih.gov
This is the home page of the National Institute on Drug Abuse.

www.undcp.org

This is the home page of the United Nations Office on Drugs and Crime.

www.rand.org/multi/dprc

This is the home page for the Drug Policy Research Center at the RAND Institute.

www.DrugWatch.org

This is the Web site for Drug Watch International.

www.ojp.usdoj.gov/bjs/drugs.htm

This Web site provides statistics on drugs and crime from the Bureau of Justice Statistics.

www.samhsa.gov

This is the home page of the Substance Abuse and Mental Health Services Administration.

www.whitehousedrugpolicy.gov

This is the home page of the Office of National Drug Control Policy.

www.lindesmith.org

This is the home page of the Drug Policy Alliance, an organization working to end the "war on drugs."

www.mpp.org

This is the home page of the Marijuana Policy Project, a nonprofit organization in the District of Columbia with the goal of providing the marijuana law reform movement with full-time lobbying on the federal level.

www.sadd.org

This is the home page of Students Against Destructive Decisions, a peer leadership organization dedicated to preventing underage drinking and drug use.

www.cops.usdoj.gov/pdf/e05021552.pdf

This PDF file contains one of the *Problem-Oriented Guides for Police* that is published by the U.S. Department of Justice. This guide focuses on the issue of street prostitution.

www.prostitutionprocon.org

ProCon.org is a nonprofit organization that focuses on education and presents the pros and cons of various controversial issues, including the legalization of prostitution.

www.bayswan.org/penet.html

This is the home page of the Prostitutes' Education Network, which discusses rights and issues relating to sex workers.

http://feminism.eserver.org/gender/sex-work

This is a link to the section on the Feminism and Women's studies site that includes articles on prostitution, pornography, and sex work.

http://prostitutionresearch.com

This is the Web site of Prostitution Research & Education.

Student Study Guide Questions

True/False

_____   1. During the nineteenth century, the use of illegal drugs was widespread throughout all levels of society.

_____   2. The cost of enforcing drug laws is a direct cost of illegal drug use.

_____   3. Marijuana is nonaddictive.

_____   4. Narcotics are physically addictive.

_____   5. Most inhalants are easily available.

_____   6. According to the DEA, most heroin in the United States originates in Asia.

_____   7. Committing a violent crime while under the influence of an illegal drug is an example of a drug-related crime.

_____   8. The Mollen Commission studied police corruption in New York City.

_____   9. The Narcotic Control Act required the complete removal of heroin from all medicines.

_____ 10. The Anti-Drug Abuse Act denied federal benefits to federal drug convicts.

_____ 11. Interdiction is an international drug-control policy.

_____ 12. The cost of the "war on drugs" has been decreasing in recent years.

_____ 13. Decriminalization involves eliminating the laws and criminal penalties associated with the production, sale, distribution, and possession of controlled substances.

_____ 14. The U.S. Supreme Court has prohibited the use of medical marijuana.

_____ 15. Both male clients and women providing sexual service may be charged with and convicted of the offense of prostitution.

_____ 16. Prostitution was legal in ancient Greece.

_____ 17. House or brothel prostitutes are common throughout the United States.

_____ 18. The majority of "johns" have attended college.

Fill in the Blank

19. _____ substances were widely accepted during the hippie movement of the 1960s.

20. Deaths resulting directly from drug consumption are known as _____ deaths.

21. _____ are used illegally by people trying to produce feelings of competence and power and a state of excitability.

22. Research suggests that _____ can be used in the treatment of glaucoma.

23. LSD falls into the _____ family of drugs.

24. Visiting numerous physicians to collect large quantities of prescribed medicines is known as _____.

25. Major heroin and cocaine trafficking routes are sometimes called _____.

26. All drugs could be bought and sold in the United States without restriction prior to the year _____.

27. The Pure Food and Drug Act was passed in _____.

28. The _____ Act required anyone dealing in drugs such as opium and cocaine to register with the federal government and pay a small annual tax.

29. The _____ Act mandated Prohibition.

30. The _____ Act effectively outlawed marijuana.

31. The Narcotic Control Act made the sale of _____ to anyone under the age of 18 a capital crime.

32. _____ involves the elimination of the laws and associated criminal penalties that prohibit the production, sale, distribution, and possession of controlled substances.

33. The _____ works for an escort service.

34. The common name for a prostitute's client is _____.

35. Prostitution has recently been redefined as _____.

36. _____ would significantly reduce the criminal penalties associated with prostitution.

Multiple Choice

37. During the late-nineteenth century, which of the following people would have been most likely to be abusing drugs (other than opium)?
    a. An upper-class merchant
    b. A servant
    c. An artist
    d. A factory worker

38. _____ is the leading cause of death of Hispanic men between the ages of 25 and 44.
    a. Drug overdose
    b. Cancer
    c. AIDS
    d. Homicide

39. Which of the following is *not* an indirect cost of illegal drug use?
    a. The cost to the criminal justice system of investigating crimes committed for drug money
    b. Lost property values due to drug-related neighborhood crime
    c. The cost of enforcing drug laws
    d. The cost of medical care for injures from drug-related child abuse or neglect

40. The _____ category of drugs includes barbiturates, sedatives, and tranquilizers.
    - a. stimulant
    - b. cannabis
    - c. narcotic
    - d. depressant

41. _____ have no official legitimate use.
    - a. Narcotics
    - b. Depressants
    - c. Stimulants
    - d. Hallucinogens

42. Most cocaine entering the United States originates in
    - a. South America.
    - b. Central America.
    - c. Asia.
    - d. Mexico.

43. The Golden Triangle area is located in
    - a. South America.
    - b. Mexico.
    - c. Southeast Asia
    - d. Southwest Asia.

44. Which of the following is an example of a drug-defined crime?
    - a. A drug addict who commits a theft to obtain money to buy drugs
    - b. A drug importer who kills a rival drug dealer
    - c. A drug dealer who sells cocaine to a juvenile on the street
    - d. They are all drug-defined crimes.

45. People with criminal records are _____ likely than/as others to report being drug users.
    - a. more
    - b. less
    - c. equally
    - d. We have no information on this topic.

46. The Pure Food and Drug Act
    - a. restricted the importation and distribution of opium.
    - b. required manufacturers to list their ingredients.
    - c. controlled the sale and possession of marijuana.
    - d. outlawed the sale and distribution of medicines containing opium.

47. Which of the following was *not* one of the provisions of the Comprehensive Methamphetamine Control Act?
    a. It added iodine to the list of chemicals controlled under federal chemical diversion acts.
    b. It created new reporting requirements for distributors of products containing certain key chemicals.
    c. It increased penalties for the manufacture and possession of equipment used to make controlled substances.
    d. It allocated drug-treatment money to create state and federal programs to treat drug-addicted prisoners.

48. The _____ Act expanded the federal death penalty to include large-scale drug trafficking.
    a. Comprehensive Methamphetamine Control
    b. Comprehensive Drug Abuse Prevention and Control
    c. Violent Crime Control and Law Enforcement
    d. Controlled Substances

49. _____ strategies focus on stopping drugs from entering the United States illegally.
    a. Source control
    b. Interdiction
    c. Asset forfeiture
    d. Crop control

50. Which of the following is *not* an argument in favor of legalization?
    a. Legalization could lower the price of drugs.
    b. Legalization would reduce the opportunity for official corruption.
    c. Drug laws are enforceable.
    d. Legalization would result in increased tax revenues.

51. California's Proposition 215 legalizes
    a. the medical use of marijuana.
    b. the sale and purchase of marijuana.
    c. Both a and b
    d. Neither a nor b

52. Prostitution is legal in parts of
    a. Nevada.
    b. California.
    c. Florida.
    d. New York.

53. _____ has legalized prostitution, but advertising sex services remains illegal.
    a. Australia
    b. New Zealand
    c. The Netherlands
    d. Germany

54. Which of the following is an argument against legalization of prostitution?
    a. Legalization will free law enforcement resources to be used on more serious crimes.
    b. Legalization will expand the sex industry rather than eliminate it.
    c. Legalization will stop prostitutes from being viewed as easy targets.
    d. Legalization will stop prostitution from being forced onto the streets.

Word Search Puzzle

```
V H H B R H X X S G U P X C O D B E O B M A T I K
J V Y I P E E H R V I J L E G A L I Z A T I O N P
V C V C H X J X I G N L C I D Q Q D B T E W K O V
G Z S W A D A N G E R O U S H J B H D R Q M V I L
I Z T J R O J O N W H H Z C Y U J Y Q Q E L L E F
X Q R F M P S Y C H O A C T I V E P K S Q F I D Q
A K A F A R S H X M M K T I Z O H L Z T Y X Y E E
G I F P C S C P S F B U V F A Y J R G Y K L X P V
Q Q F G E N N Y Y I P Q Y K D D D D V I N T W J C H
V N I I U C U O J I U T F M A G D H G B P S C Z B
E I C E T M I Y U C H D Z Y M L J L E R W M Q F L
F M K U I O W R E T O E H F M W X W P X A C F C K
N T I K C C L E U D R V Q J O L E Q O G W M E D P
F V N S A A G P S Q Z A D R U G D E F I N E D R Y
R O G P L F N F N R N C S E C H W O S X S D X U Z
U X D E C R I M I N A L I Z A T I O N J T F V G A
X B Q R C Z W N L M N J D T N C G K F Z M B B R K
D P R O S T I T U T I O N G C N Z J U K D U L E O
W N A Q I G C W D J J D Z P M N B G G V S R R L N
I L Q E X X D O N T E Y L O R B C P E A B Y X A B
T L M F J B W S N Q C H G L T P J V I V B V S T L
Y O G L D K X L J Q Q I Z S D U Q X C R K C A E O
U R B K H S P H S Z U R X D Q O V L Q U O S J D G
G L J T S T P A L D D X M T G Q S Y J N P E Z D R
U V M D E S I G N E R K B I N T E R D I C T I O N
```

ADAM	Dangerous	Decriminalization	Designer	Drug defined
Drug related	HSP	Interdiction	Legalization	Pharmaceutical
Prostitution	Psychoactive	Trafficking		

Crossword Puzzle

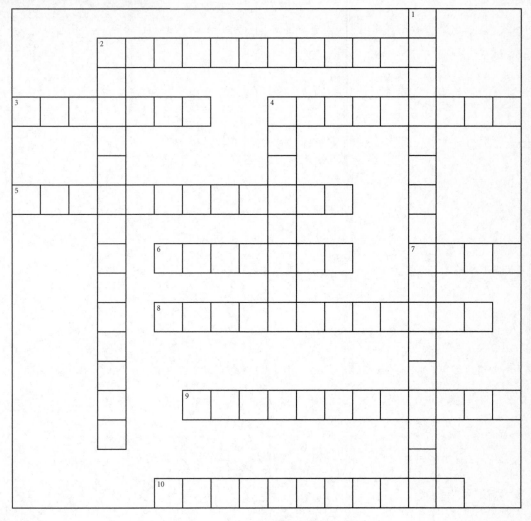

Across

2. A substance affecting the mind, mental processes, or emotions.
3. A drug-_____ crime is one in which drugs contribute to the offense.
4. A DEA term referring to drugs other than cocaine, opiates, and cannabis products.
5. Eliminating the laws that prohibit the possession and sale of controlled substances.
6. A drug-_____ crime violates the laws prohibiting or regulating the possession, use, or distribution of illegal drugs.
7. An NIJ program that tracks trends in the prevalence and types of drug use among booked arrestees in urban areas.
8. An international drug-control policy trying to stop drugs from entering the country illegally.
9. Offering one's self for hire for the purpose of engaging in sexual relations.
10. Drug _____ involves manufacturing and distributing controlled substances.

Down

1. Redefining previously criminal behaviors into regulated activities that become "ticketable" rather than "arrestable".
2. _____ diversion involves diverting legitimately manufactured controlled substances for illicit use.
4. A drug created by slightly altering the chemical makeup of other illegal drugs.

14 Technology and Crime

Learning Outcomes

After reading this chapter, students should be able to:

- Describe the link between technological advances and crime, and explain how technology can be used by both criminals and crime fighters
- Describe how technology can provide criminal opportunity, and use computer crime as an illustration
- Provide a profile of computer criminals, including a history of hacking and a description of cyberspace
- Define *identity theft*, describe how identities can be stolen, and explain what can be done to reduce the crime's negative impact on its victims
- Describe some of today's technologies that are being used to fight crime
- Explain what is being done today to combat computer crime and to secure the Internet
- Identify some of the personal freedoms that are threatened by today's need for advanced security, and explain the nature of that threat

Chapter Outline

Dealing with Computer Criminals
Securing the Internet
Policy Issues: Personal Freedoms in the Information Age

Chapter Summary

This chapter discusses the links between technology and crime. Technology, which facilitates new forms of criminal behavior, can be used both by criminals and by those who enforce the law. Because of the increasing value of information, high-tech criminals have taken a variety of routes to obtain illegitimate access to computerized information. Some criminals may focus simply on destroying or altering information rather than copying it. Technically, computer crime is defined as any violation of a federal or state computer crime statute. The text discusses several typologies of computer crime. Some authors use the term *cybercrime* to refer to crimes involving the use of computers or the manipulation of digital data. One example of cybercrime is phone phreaking, which involves the illegitimate use of dial-up access codes and other restricted technical information to avoid long-distance charges or to steal cellular telephone numbers and access codes. In addition, some computer crime is malicious rather than being committed for financial gain; this includes the creation and transmission of computer viruses, worms, and other malicious forms of programming code.

Originally, most jurisdictions in the United States attempted to prosecute unauthorized computer access under preexisting property crime statutes. However, today, all states and the federal government have developed computer crime statutes specifically applicable to invasive activities aimed at illegally accessing stored information. There is a variety of federal statutes of relevance to crimes committed with or against computer equipment and software. One of the most controversial has been the Computer Decency Act (CDA), signed into law in 1996, which focused on protecting minors from harmful material on the Internet by making it a crime to knowingly transmit obscene or indecent material to a recipient under the age of 18. However, the ACLU filed suit against the federal government, challenging the constitutionality of the CDA's provisions relating to the transmission of obscene material to minors. After a federal district court ruled that the provisions violated the First Amendment guarantees of free speech, the case was appealed to the U.S. Supreme Court, which upheld the lower court's ruling in the 1997 case of *Reno* v. *ACLU*. Individual state laws are rarely modeled after federal legislation and generally vary greatly among states. Some experts distinguish among several categories of crimes involving computers, including computer crime, computer-related crime, and computer abuse.

Many computer criminals come from the hacker subculture. Hackers and hacker identities are a product of cyberspace, which exists only within electronic networks. The text discusses a typology of hackers that is based on psychological characteristics. In addition, some high-tech crimes are committed by professional criminals who use technology to commit serious crimes, such as the theft of money. The World Wide Web may also be used to facilitate criminal activity, such as the computerized transmission of illegal pornography among pedophiles. Computer crime also shares a number of characteristics with white-collar crime.

Identity theft involves the misuse of another individual's personal information to commit fraud, and generally is divided into two broad categories: existing account fraud and new account fraud. Identity theft creates not only direct costs but also a variety of indirect costs to businesses and individual victims. In 1998, identity theft became a federal crime. The "life cycle" of identity theft appears to have three stages. The first occurs when the thief attempts to acquire a victim's personal information; the second is when the thief attempts to misuse this information; and the third occurs when the thief has completed the crime. Federal offices charged with combating identity theft have proposed strategies for preventing and responding to the crime.

Technology helps both criminals and criminal justice personnel; law enforcement capabilities and criminally useful technologies usually leapfrog each other. Key technology in law enforcement service today includes traffic radar, computer databases of known offenders, machine-based expert systems, cellular communications, electronic eavesdropping, DNA analysis, and less-than-lethal weapons. DNA profiling has become an important tool for criminal justice, and all states have passed legislation requiring convicted offenders to provide samples for DNA databasing.

Computers themselves may serve as tools in the fight against crime. Technologies such as AFIS (automated fingerprint identification systems) and online criminal information services (NCIC, VICAP, etc.) facilitate the work of law enforcement agents. Expert systems that attempt to duplicate the decision-making processes used by skilled investigators may be used in offender profiling. Combating computer crime necessarily involves a realistic threat analysis that identifies organizational perils so that strategies to deal with them can be introduced. One powerful tool is the audit trail. Currently, few police departments have specialized computer crime units or personnel skilled in the investigation of computer crime, and many place a low priority on the investigation of computer crime.

The Internet is the world's largest computer network; its growth has encouraged hackers and computer criminals to attack it through the creation and development of programs such as viruses and worms. Because information and property can be transmitted through data networks, cybercriminals are not affected by national boundaries, nor do they have to be anywhere near the location of the victim to commit crimes. However, law enforcement agencies are still affected by geographic boundaries and may still have to deal with the difficulties of international cooperation.

Any effective policy for dealing with computer criminals must recognize various issues associated with personal freedoms and individual rights and must address the issues of deterrence. Sanctions that may be effective in deterring high-tech offenders include confiscating equipment used to commit a computer crime, limiting the offender's use of computers, and restricting the offender's freedom to accept jobs involving computers. One key policy issue is whether the First Amendment's protection of free speech applies to electronic communications. Private groups such as the Electronic Frontier Foundation (EFF) have been formed to focus on the protection of constitutional principles as new communications technologies emerge.

Key Concepts

Audit trail: A sequential record of computer system activities that enables auditors to reconstruct, review, and examine the sequence of states and activities surrounding each event in one or more related transactions from inception to output of final results back to inception.

Communications Decency Act: A federal statute signed into law in 1996, the CDA is Title 5 of the federal Telecommunications Act of 1996 (Public Law 104–104, 110 Stat. 56). The law sought to protect minors from harmful material on the Internet and a portion of the CDA criminalized the knowing transmission of obscene or indecent messages to any recipient under 18 years of age. In 1997, however, in the case of *Reno* v. *ACLU* (521 US 844), the U.S. Supreme Court found the bulk of the CDA to be unconstitutional, ruling that it contravenes First Amendment free speech guarantees.

Computer abuse: Any unlawful incident associated with computer technology in which a victim suffered or could have suffered loss or in which a perpetrator by intention made or could have made gain.

Computer crime: Any violation of a federal or state computer crime statute. See also **cybercrime**.

Computer-related crime: Any illegal act for which knowledge of computer technology is involved in its perpetration, investigation, or prosecution.

Computer virus: A set of computer instructions that propagates copies or versions of itself into computer programs or data when it is executed.

Cyber Security Enhancement Act: Part of the Homeland Security Act of 2002, this federal law directed the U.S. sentencing commission to take several specific factors into account in creating new sentencing guidelines for computer criminals.

Cybercrime: Crime committed with the use of computers or via the manipulation of digital forms of data. See also **computer crime**.

Cyberspace: The computer-created matrix of virtual possibilities, including online services, wherein human beings interact with one another and with the technology itself.

Data encryption: The process by which information is encoded, making it unreadable to all but its intended recipients.

***Daubert* standard:**   A test of scientific acceptability applicable to the gathering of evidence in criminal cases.

DCS-1000:   A network diagnostic tool that is capable of assisting in criminal investigations by monitoring and capturing large amounts of Internet traffic. Previously called *Carnivore*.

Digital Theft Deterrence and Copyright Damages Improvement Act: Passed in 1999, this federal law (Public Law 106–160) attempted to combat software piracy and other forms of digital theft by amending Section 504(c) of the Copyright Act, thereby increasing the amount of damages that could potentially be awarded in cases of copyright infringement.

DNA profiling: The use of biological residue found at the scene of a crime for genetic comparisons in aiding the identification of criminal suspects.

Expert systems: Computer hardware and software that attempt to duplicate the decision-making processes used by skilled investigators in the analysis of evidence and in the recognition of patterns that such evidence might represent.

Hacker: A person who uses computers for exploration and exploitation.

Identity theft: The unauthorized use of another individual's personal identity to fraudulently obtain money, goods, or services; to avoid the payment of debt; or to avoid criminal prosecution.

Internet: The world's largest computer network.

No Electronic Theft Act: A 1997 federal law (Public Law 105–147) that criminalizes the willful infringement of copyrighted works, including by electronic means, even when the infringing party derives no direct financial benefit from the infringement (such as when pirated software is freely distributed online). In keeping with requirements of the NETA, the U.S. Sentencing Commission enacted amendments to its guidelines on April 6, 2000, to increase penalties associated with electronic theft.

Phishing: Pronounced "fishing." An Internet-based scam to steal valuable information, such as credit card numbers, social security numbers, user IDs, and passwords.

Phone phreak: A person who uses switched, dialed-access telephone services for exploration and exploitation.

Software piracy: The unauthorized and illegal copying of software programs.

TEMPEST: A standard developed by the U.S. government that requires that electromagnetic emanations from computers designated as "secure" be below levels that would allow radio receiving equipment to "read" the data being computed.

Threat analysis: A complete and thorough assessment of the kinds of perils facing an organization. Also called *risk analysis*.

Questions for Review

1. How does advancing technology produce new forms of crime? How does it affect crime fighting?
2. How does technology provide criminal opportunity? Why does advancing technology sometimes necessitate new criminal laws?
3. What different types of computer criminals does this chapter describe? Why do some hackers commit criminal mischief?
4. What is identity theft? How can identities be stolen? What can be done to reduce the impact of identity theft on victims?
5. What new technologies are being used in today's fight against crime?
6. What is being done to combat computer crime and to secure the Internet today?
7. What are some of the personal freedoms that are threatened by today's need for advanced security?

Questions for Reflection

1. This book emphasizes a social problems versus social responsibility theme. Which perspective best explains the involvement of capable individuals in criminal activity necessitating high-tech skills? What is the best way to deal with such criminals?
2. What is the difference between high-tech crime and traditional forms of criminal activity? Will the high-tech crimes of today continue to be the high-tech crimes of tomorrow? Why?
3. What forms of high-tech crime can you imagine that this chapter has not discussed? Describe each briefly.
4. Do you believe that high-tech crimes will eventually surpass the abilities of enforcement agents to prevent or solve them? Why?
5. What different kinds of high-tech offenders can you imagine? What is the best way to deal with each type of offender? Give reasons for your answers.

Student Exercises

Activity #1

Select three theories that you have discussed in previous chapters and discuss how each of these might explain the actions of high-tech offenders.

Activity #2

Visit a local, county, or state police department in your area and find out how they handle cases of computer crime.

Criminology Today on the Web

www.eff.org

This is the home page of the Electronic Frontier Foundation.

www.polcyb.org

This is the home page of the Society for the Policing of Cyberspace.

www.usdoj.gov/criminal/cybercrime/index.html

This is the home page of the U.S. Department of Justice Computer Crime and Intellectual Property Section.

www.fraud.org/welcome.htm

This is the home page of the National Fraud Information Center, which includes information on Internet fraud.

www.siia.net

This is the home page of the Software and Information Industry Association.

www.cnn.com/US/9703/cda.scotus

This CNN site provides information on the case of *Reno* v. *ACLU* and the history of the debate over the Communications Decency Act.

www.cpsr.org

This is the home page of Computer Professionals for Social Responsibility.

www.howstuffworks.com/virus.htm

This Web site provides information on how computer viruses actually work.

Student Study Guide Questions

True/False

_____ 1. The path of direct access to computer information is generally used by office workers violating positions of trust.

_____ 2. Cybercrime involves any violation of a federal or state computer crime statute.

_____ 3. Illegal hacking is an example of a computer manipulation crime.

_____ 4. According to the Software and Information Industry Association, softlifting involves illegally duplicating and distributing copyrighted software in a form designed to make it appear legitimate.

_____ 5. The electronic theft of cellular telephone numbers and access codes is known as phishing.

_____ 6. The creation and transmission of computer viruses is committed for financial gain.

_____ 7. The Communications Decency Act criminalized the willful infringement of copyrighted works by electronic means.

_____ 8. *Computer-related crime* is defined as the violation of a federal or state computer crime statute.

_____ 9. Cyberpunk is the place where computers and people interact with one another.

_____ 10. The primary motivation of the average hacker is financial profit.

_____ 11. Scamps are malicious hackers who intend to damage computer records.

_____ 12. Identity theft involves the misuse of another individual's personal information to commit fraud.

_____ 13. Shoulder surfing occurs when Internet users reply to spam.

_____ 14. The "Spiderman snare" is a discolike strobe light that quickly disorients human targets.

_____ 15. The *Daubert* standard deals with the application of the laws requiring convicted offenders to provide DNA samples.

_____ 16. Most police departments today are prepared to effectively investigate computer crimes.

_____ 17. The best way to deter computer offenders is to incarcerate them.

_____ 18. Cybercriminals do not need to come into direct contact with victims.

Fill in the Blank

19. Computer _____ involves remote access to targeted machines.

20. The TEMPEST program was developed by the U.S. Department of _____.

21. The term used by the computer underground for pirated software is _____.

22. _____ is a form of software piracy that involves purchasing a single licensed copy of software and loading the same copy onto several computers.

23. A computer _____ is a program designed to invade a computer system and modify the way it operates or alter the information it stores.

24. Early attempts at prosecuting unauthorized computer access used preexisting _____ crime statutes.

25. The Communications Decency Act was challenged on the grounds that it contravened the _____ Amendment to the U.S. Constitution.

26. Computer hackers and hacker identities are products of _____.

27. Hackers who intend no overt harm but just have a sense of fun are known as _____.

28. _____ see hacking itself as a game.

29. The misuse of another individual's personal information to commit fraud is known as _____.

30. _____ account fraud occurs when thieves obtain account information involving accounts that are already open.

31. In some jurisdictions, _____ systems involve computers prompting police dispatchers for important information, which allows them to distinguish locations within a city.

32. The _____ police were the first national police force in the world to begin routine collection of DNA samples from anyone involved in a serious crime.

33. _____ allows investigators to use computers to match a suspect's fingerprints against stored records.

34. The FBI's National Center for the Analysis of Violent Crime is an example of a(n) _____ system.

35. _____ involves a complete and thorough assessment of the perils facing an organization.

36. The FBI's National Computer Crime Squad investigates violations of the federal _____ Act.

Multiple Choice

37. The person most likely to invade a computer is a(n)
    a. hacker.
    b. unauthorized user.
    c. current employee
    d. skilled computer amateur.

38. Using a computer to create a database of drug buyers falls within which of David Carter's categories of computer crime?
    a. Crimes in which computers serve as targets
    b. Crimes in which computers serve as the instrumentality of the crime
    c. Crimes in which the computer is incidental to other crimes
    d. Crimes associated with the prevalence of computers

39. According to the Software and Information Industry Association, _____ involves making unauthorized copies of copyrighted software available to others over the Internet.
    a. softlifting
    b. Internet piracy
    c. renting
    d. OEM unbundling

40. According to the Software and Information Industry Association, _____ involves selling stand-alone software that was intended to be bundled with specific accompanying hardware.
    a. softlifting
    b. software counterfeiting
    c. renting
    d. OEM unbundling

41. The goal of _____ is generally to encourage the end user to purchase hardware from a specific hardware vendor.

     a. hard disk loading
     b. renting
     c. OEM unbundling
     d. softlifting

42. Phone phreaking is an example of the _____ category of computer crime.

     a. internal computer crime
     b. telecommunications
     c. computer manipulation crimes
     d. support of criminal enterprises

43. _____ is/are an example of the "information theft" category of computer crime.

     a. Viruses
     b. Hacking
     c. Software piracy
     d. Money laundering

44. The _____ Act criminalized the willful infringement of copyrighted works.

     a. No Electronic Theft
     b. Communications Decency
     c. Digital Theft Deterrence and Copyright Damages
     d. National Stolen Property

45. _____ is defined as any incident without color of right associated with computer technology in which a victim suffered or could have suffered loss and/or a perpetrator intentionally made or could have made gain.

     a. Computer crime
     b. Computer-related crime
     c. Computer abuse
     d. Cybercrime

46. _____ are hackers who are fascinated by the evolving technology of telecommunications and explore it without knowing exactly what they will find.

     a. Pioneers
     b. Scamps
     c. Explorers
     d. Addicts

47. _____ are malicious hackers who deliberately cause damage with no apparent gain for themselves.

     a. Explorers
     b. Scamps
     c. Game players
     d. Vandals

48. Which type of identity theft is more common?
    a. New account fraud
    b. Existing account fraud
    c. Softlifting
    d. OEM unbundling

49. Which is *not* one of the components of an effective national strategy for preventing and responding to identity theft, according to the Office of Community Oriented Policing Services?
    a. Legislation
    b. Public awareness campaigns
    c. Information protection
    d. Victim restitution programs

50. In the case of _____, the U.S. Supreme Court held that for scientific evidence to be admissible in court, the test or procedure must be generally accepted by the relevant scientific community.
    a. *Frye* v. *United States*
    b. *Reno* v. *ACLU*
    c. *Daubert* v. *Merrell Dow Pharmaceuticals, Inc.*
    d. None of the above

51. Bulletproof software, which compares a bullet's ballistic characteristics with those stored in a database, was developed by the
    a. FBI.
    b. Police Executive Research Forum.
    c. Bureau of Alcohol, Tobacco and Firearms.
    d. Bureau of Justice Statistics.

52. A(n) _____ records the activities of computer operators surrounding each event in a transaction.
    a. threat analysis
    b. audit trail
    c. DNA profile
    d. expert systems analysis

53. Which of the following is *not* one of the three sanctions that may be especially effective in deterring high-tech offenders?
    a. Limiting the offender's use of computers
    b. Restricting the offender's freedom to accept jobs that involve computers
    c. Confiscating the equipment used to commit a computer crime
    d. Providing training in socially acceptable ways to use a computer

54. The _____ was created by President Clinton in 1996.
    a. Commission on Critical Infrastructure Protection
    b. National Infrastructure Protection Center
    c. President's Working Group on Unlawful Conduct on the Internet
    d. National Cybercrime Training Partnership

Word Search Puzzle

```
Z X U Q M G U K N L L A D A U B E R T H P I L T I
I N G V I K F E R A P Z F A R N B G K Z E H I V D
G W G Z I N T E R N E T C A N Z T N V R U N L K E
E P Z S U I S O B X J V H A C K E R K S F U P D N
Y E A Q H N R V A E N C R Y P T I O N G K M U U T
J W T I M L O W Y P D L E G A Q V R L G V P R F I
M V J E O U M C Y I W U I P C B I C L Y V M Z C T
T Y K V F P V F M M C S A N F H R I B U X F I Q Y
G Z X F A L D A Z E R F U C R S U T B Q Q J B O Y
B D U H H O P B K B Q Q J M P K S B U I N M D J U
P C O R P B Y Z V A P H O N E P H R E A K K N K J
H P V O M V G D U D H X X Z N G K E P I R A C Y T
I U G T Z C T Z H C F T S O F V S S I S R T X U I
S O M O I I K S X N Z Z Z F S O F T W A R E W J F
H T A E X K C O M P U T E R M L P D W D B U Q V X
I V S W E I D Z T H R E A T L V B O R Q H J T F V
N F X N N X H S V R I T R H S M W I E A R E K S P
G V G U T I J I X T Q X T Z R Y Q S L U I S S Y E
Q X U H I I P C Y B E R S P A C E M K D D O Z T T
B F I U R S X F L A S H F Y Y D I I A I G D R F E
W P X X U F I S O V V H N S T U O P H T P B M Q M
D Q H O I G U R V C Y B E R C R I M E F H X F Z P
F R Q D R Z V G W L Q V U Z X Q L D H E H C F K E
G Q Q X X C X L S X D C G S Z H N D U A K D V M S
N S H W U Q L O W W T H J Q F T K K F R B I Y L T
```

Audit	Computer	Cybercrime	Cyberspace	Daubert	Encryption
Hacker	Identity	Internet	Phishing	Piracy	Phone phreak
Software	TEMPEST	Threat	Virus		

Crossword Puzzle

Across

3. A person who uses computers for exploration and exploitation.
5. Crime committed with the use of computers or via the manipulation of digital forms of data.
7. _____ analysis is a thorough assessment of the kinds of perils facing an organization.
8. A phone _____ uses telephone services for exploration and exploitation.
9. The _____ standard is a test of scientific acceptability of evidence gathering in criminal cases.
10. An Internet-based scam to steal valuable information.
11. The world's largest computer network.

Down

1. A set of computer instructions that propagates copies or versions of itself into computer programs.
2. The computer-created matrix of virtual possibilities wherein human beings interact with one another and with the technology itself.
4. A(n) _____ trail is a sequential record of computer system activities.
6. The process by which information is encoded.
7. A government regulating electromagnetic emanations from secure computers.

15

Globalization and Terrorism

Learning Outcomes

After reading this chapter, students should be able to:

- Define *globalization* and tell how it impacts contemporary criminal and terrorist activity
- Explain comparative criminology and describe the advantages of a comparative approach to the study of crime and criminals
- Define *terrorism*, and identify various methods of terrorism and possible methods for the control of terrorism

Chapter Outline

Introduction
Globalization
    Transnational Crimes
Comparative Criminology
    Ethnocentrism
    Issues in Reporting
Terrorism
    International Terrorism
    Domestic Terrorism
    Cyberterrorism
    Terrorism and Technology
    The War on Terrorism
    Terrorism Commissions and Reports
    Countering the Terrorist Threat
    The Future of Terrorism

Chapter Summary

This chapter focuses on two topics: globalization and terrorism. Globalization is "a process of social homogenization by which the experiences of everyday life, marked by the diffusion of commodities and ideas, can foster a standardization of cultural expressions around the world." Globalization is forcing policymakers to focus on criminal activity in other parts of the world, particularly transnational organized crime, which is unlawful activity undertaken and supported by organized criminal groups operating across national boundaries.

Transnational crimes range from fraudulent e-mail and phishing schemes to drug running, international trade in weapons of mass destruction, sex tourism, and illegal trafficking in human beings and human organs. Human smuggling and trafficking are some of the fastest growing areas of international criminal activity today. Human smuggling refers to illegal immigration in which a criminal agent receives payment to help a person illegally and clandestinely cross a border. Human trafficking involves the exploitation of unwilling or unwitting people through force, coercion, threat, or deception, and includes human rights abuses, such as debt bondage, deprivation of liberty, or lack of control over freedom and labor. Trafficking is often undertaken for purposes of sexual exploitation or labor exploitation. A wide variety of federal immigration and trafficking legislation has been enacted in an effort to place controls on immigration.

The globalization of crime has led to a renewed interest in comparative criminology, the cross-national study of crime. The globalization of knowledge is beginning to impact theory formation and the development of crime control policies in the United States. A key issue is ethnocentrism, or culture-centeredness. Despite interest in comparing crime rates across countries, there are a number of difficulties, including definitional differences; diverse crime reporting practices; and political, social, economic, and other influences on the reporting of statistics to international agencies.

Terrorism is defined in this chapter as "premeditated, politically motivated violence perpetrated against noncombatant targets by subnational groups or clandestine agents, usually intended to influence an audience." Terrorist acts are distinguished from other violent crimes by the political motivation or ideology of the offender. Various typologies of terrorist activities have been developed. The United States has to deal with both international and domestic terrorism. A recent development is that of cyberterrorism, which uses technology to plan and carry out terrorist attacks against the economic, business, and military infrastructure of a country. A number of commissions have been formed to study terrorism and the country's preparedness to deal with terrorist threats. A variety of new laws, which have been passed in an effort to prevent terrorism, restrict various freedoms commonly taken for granted by most Americans.

Key Concepts

Comparative criminologist: A criminologist involved in the cross-national study of crime.

Comparative criminology: The cross-national study of crime.

Cyberterrorism: A form of terrorism that makes use of high technology, especially computer technology and the Internet, in the planning and carrying out of terrorist attacks.

Domestic terrorism: The unlawful use of force or violence by a group or an individual who is based and operates entirely within the United States and its territories without foreign direction and whose acts are directed at elements of the U.S. government or population.

Ethnocentrism: The phenomenon of "culture-centeredness" by which one uses one's own culture as a benchmark against which to judge all other patterns of behavior.

Foreign terrorist organization (FTO):   A foreign organization that engages in terrorist activity that threatens the security of U.S. nationals or the national security of the United States and that is so designated by the U.S. secretary of state.

Globalization: A process of social homogenization by which the experiences of everyday life, marked by the diffusion of commodities and ideas, can foster a standardization of cultural expressions around the world.

Human smuggling: Illegal immigration in which an agent is involved for payment to help a person cross a border clandestinely.

Infrastructure: The basic facilities, services, and installations needed for the functioning of a community or society, such as transportation and communications systems, water and power lines, and public institutions, including schools, post offices, and prisons.

International terrorism: The unlawful use of force or violence by a group or an individual who has a connection to a foreign power or whose activities transcend national boundaries against people or property to intimidate or coerce a government, the civilian population, or any segment thereof in furtherance of political or social objectives.

Sex trafficking: The recruitment, harboring, transportation, provision, or obtaining of a person for the purpose of a commercial sex act.

Terrorism: Premeditated, politically motivated violence perpetrated against noncombatant targets by subnational groups or clandestine agents, usually intended to influence an audience.

Trafficking in persons (TIP): The exploitation of unwilling or unwitting people through force, coercion, threat, or deception.

Transnational organized crime: Unlawful activity undertaken and supported by organized criminal groups operating across national boundaries.

Questions for Review

1. What is globalization? How does it impact criminal activity in today's world? In the United States? How does it affect terrorism?
2. What is comparative criminology? What are the advantages of a comparative approach in the study of criminology?
3. What is terrorism? What types of terrorism does this chapter discuss?

Questions for Reflection

1. What are the advantages of a comparative perspective in criminology? Are there any disadvantages? If so, what are they?
2. What types of terrorism has this chapter identified? Are there any it might have missed? If so, what are they?
3. Has the "war against terrorism" affected you personally? If so, how?
4. Has the average American had to sacrifice any rights or freedoms in the fight against terrorism? If so, what rights or freedoms have been sacrificed?
5. Some people say that the only way to secure freedom is to curtail it during times of national crisis. Can this be true? Why?

Student Exercises

Activity #1

Your instructor will assign you a specific country. Write a short paper profiling the terrorist problem in that country. Your paper should include (but is not limited to) a discussion of the various terrorist organizations active within the country, describe various terrorist attacks in that country, and review the antiterrorism laws (if any) that are in force. The Terrorism Research Center's Web site (provided in the next section) may be a useful source of information for this activity.

Activity #2

Your instructor will assign you a specific terrorist group. Write a short paper profiling that group. Include information on the group's formation and history; its ideology, mission, and goals; and the terrorist activities in which the group has engaged to further its objectives.

Criminology Today on the Web

www.lib.umich.edu/govdocs/usterror.html

This is a link to the University of Michigan Documents Center, which has a wealth of information on the 9/11 terrorist attacks and the aftermath.

www.terrorism.com/index.php

This is the home page of the Terrorism Research Center.

www.cfr.org/issue/135/terrorism.html

This is a link to the terrorism section of the Council on Foreign Relations.

www.fema.gov/hazard/terrorism

This is a link to a fact sheet on terrorism presented by FEMA.

www.dhs.gov/index.shtm

This is the home page of the U.S. Department of Homeland Security.

www.fbi.gov/terrorinfo/counterrorism/waronterrorhome.htm

This is the FBI's page on counterterrorism and terrorism.

www.nctc.gov

This is the home page of the National Counterterrorism Center.

www.globalpolicy.org/globaliz/index.htm

This is a link to the Global Policy Forum's page on globalization.

www.sociology.emory.edu/globalization/books.html

This is a link to the Globalization Web site, which contains a wide selection of links to sites that focus on the issue of globalization.

www.rohan.sdsu.edu/faculty/rwinslow/index.html

This is a link to the Crime and Society Web site, which provides users with a comparative criminology tour of the world.

Student Study Guide Questions

True/False

_____ 1. Human smuggling generally occurs with the consent of the persons being smuggled.

_____ 2. Trafficking involves some element of force, fraud, or coercion.

_____ 3. The Immigration and Naturalization Service was established by the Immigration Act of 1924.

_____ 4. Sex trafficking involves inducing a commercial sex act by force, fraud, or coercion.

_____ 5. Comparative criminology involves comparing crime rates in different states within the United States.

_____ 6. Social and political contexts may be reflected in crime statistics.

_____ 7. Terrorism is motivated by financial gain.

_____ 8. Terrorism frequently is an impulsive act of rage.

_____ 9. State-sponsored terrorist groups are deliberately used by radical states as foreign policy tools.

_____ 10. Experts suggest that the risk of international terrorism is decreasing and that the United States will suffer from fewer incidents of international terrorism.

_____ 11. The anthrax letter incident in 2001 and 2002 is an example of international terrorism.

_____ 12. Cyberterrorism uses the Internet and the World Wide Web to plan and carry out terrorist attacks.

_____ 13. The Transportation Security Administration is part of the Department of Homeland Security.

_____ 14. The Bremmer Commission was formed as a result of the events of September 11, 2001.

_____ 15. FTOs are so designated by the U.S. secretary of state.

_____ 16. The Department of Homeland Security has the authority to designate selected foreign governments as state sponsors of international terrorism.

_____ 17. The most active state sponsor of terrorism in the world is Cuba.

_____ 18. U.S. antiterrorist policy today focuses primarily on individuals who are not affiliated with established terrorist organizations.

Fill in the Blank

19. _____ organized crime involves criminal groups operating across national boundaries.

20. _____ can be compared to a modern-day form of slavery.

21. Under U.S. law, if a person induced to perform a commercial sex act is under the age of _____, it is considered trafficking even if force, fraud, or coercion is not involved.

22. _____ criminology is the study of crime on a cross-national level.

23. _____ is the phenomenon of culture-centeredness.

24. In _____, obtaining information through face-to-face questioning is considered to be offensive.

25. Terrorism is usually aimed at _____.

26. _____ terrorists are revolutionaries who seek to overthrow all established forms of government.

27. _____ terrorism involves the unlawful use of force or violence by a group or individual with a connection to a foreign power or whose activities transcend national boundaries.

28. The terrorist bombing of the federal building in Oklahoma City is an example of _____ terrorism.

29. _____ targets the virtual world.

30. The private Internet being created by the U.S. government is known as _____.

31. _____ seeks to disperse destructive or disease-producing biological active agents among the population.

32. The first director of the Department of Homeland Security was _____.

33. The Department of Homeland Security includes _____ directorates or departmental divisions.

34. The _____ Directorate within the DHS works to ensure that the country is prepared for, and able to recover from, terrorist attacks.

35. The _____ holds the authority to designate a group as an FTO.

36. A key issue relating to international terrorism is a trend toward the proliferation of _____.

Multiple Choice

37. _____ involves illegal immigration in which an agent receives payment to help someone cross a border clandestinely.
    a. Transnational organized crime
    b. Human smuggling
    c. Trafficking in persons
    d. Globalization

38. Which is *not* an underlying condition giving rise to trafficking in persons and human smuggling?

        a. Extreme poverty
        b. Lack of economic opportunity
        c. Political uncertainty
        d. Use of illegal drugs

39. The _____ limited the number of immigrants who could be admitted to the United States from any one country and barred immigration from specific parts of the Asia-Pacific Triangle.

        a. Chinese Exclusion Act
        b. Trafficking Victims Protection Act
        c. Homeland Security Act
        d. Immigration Act

40. The Immigration Act of 1924 barred immigration into the United States from all but which of the following countries?

        a. Cambodia
        b. The Philippines
        c. Mexico
        d. Laos

41. Which act established the Human Smuggling and Trafficking Center within the U.S. State Department?

        a. The Trafficking Victims Protection Reauthorization Act
        b. The Immigration and Nationality Act
        c. The Intelligence Reform and Terrorism Prevention Act
        d. The Homeland Security Act

42. A(n) _____ criminologist is involved in the cross-national study of crime.

        a. ethnocentric
        b. classical
        c. biosocial
        d. comparative

43. Which of the following international agencies regularly collects crime statistics from a large number of countries?

        a. The United Nations
        b. The International Criminal Court
        c. The International Court of Justice
        d. None of the above

44. An act of terrorism is distinguished from a violent criminal act by

        a. the location of the act.
        b. the type of behavior involved.
        c. the motivation of the offender.
        d. All of the above

45. Which of the following is not a characteristic of terrorism?
    a. It is premeditated or planned.
    b. It is aimed at civilians.
    c. It is perpetrated by the army of a country.
    d. It is politically motivated.

46. _____ terrorists want to destroy economies based on free enterprise and replace them with socialist or communist economic systems.
    a. Left-wing
    b. Right-wing
    c. State-sponsored
    d. Anarchist

47. _____ terrorism refers only to acts of terrorism that occur outside the United States.
    a. Domestic
    b. International
    c. Anarchist
    d. Foreign

48. Which of the following is an example of a right-wing terrorist group?
    a. al-Qaeda
    b. Neo-Nazis
    c. The Irish Republican Army
    d. The Japanese Red Army

49. _____ is a form of terrorism that uses high technology in the planning and carrying out of terrorist attacks.
    a. GovNet
    b. Bioterrorism
    c. Cyberterrorism
    d. Cyberspace

50. The _____ was formed by President Clinton to study critical components of the country's infrastructure.
    a. President's Commission on Critical Infrastructure Protection
    b. Critical Infrastructure Assurance Office
    c. Department of Homeland Security
    d. National Infrastructure Protection Center

51. Which of the following was *not* amended by the USA PATRIOT Act?
    a. The Bank Secrecy Act
    b. The Electronic Communications Privacy Act
    c. The Family Education Rights and Privacy Act
    d. The Sarbanes-Oxley Act

52. The _____ Directorate within the Department of Homeland Security is responsible for research and development efforts.

      a. Science and Technology
      b. Management
      c. Information Analysis and Infrastructure Protection
      d. Emergency Preparedness and Response

53. The National Commission on Terrorism is also known as the _____ Commission.

      a. Gilmore
      b. Bremmer
      c. Hart-Rudman
      d. 9/11

54. Which of the following is *not* a consequence of designation as a foreign terrorist organization?

      a. It is illegal for a person in the United States or subject to U.S. jurisdiction to provide funds or material support to a foreign terrorist organization.
      b. Representatives and some members of designated foreign terrorist organizations may be denied visas or kept from entering the United States if they are aliens.
      c. U.S. financial institutions are required to block funds of designated foreign terrorist organizations and their agents and report the blockage to the U.S. Department of the Treasury.
      d. Members of designated foreign terrorist organizations may be deported by the U.S. Department of State without review.

Word Search Puzzle

```
D T Q L M N G F H Z V C Y B E R T E R R O R I S M
J V A H E M S R C G M I A I S C I E D X Q T Z I C
D G Z F Q H G D U R N A O C O V O T E Z Y Z D I Y
W N M Y Q B Z F T O H J P M M T F H C D V F E X H
V B K H R F G Z T C K F X S M R B N O X V W Q A N
Y M S I I N T E R N A T I O N A L O M Z S D S A Q
G R P P P J V U P C K F R D R O F R C P T Z W G K H
Y Z C B S G T F J J P K Y V C F F E A R E J D S T
U R H E L Q I U V G L W E N I I I N R X K O B Z H
X D L U Z P N U W V F P H A H C H T A U M N L Q C
K W S T Y Z F I I N P D B Y V K M R T X O Z T W P
R F A V X B R C J Q G P M C H I P I I P U X E U V
S O G B L Z A Z G M L W P A P N A S V P U I S F R
M Z R G Q O S W M J T E R R C G C M E W Z M K R C
U D K B N P T G I I D N T I R R L M F X F E S P F
G J I R L A R F E A O L U C H T Q O V L B P H B Y
G P M D W F U W Y R M R J G X T H K J E A L W T O
L I T W F E C J L P E Q N X M U V D O L B K S R T
I Y M P T J T G S D S Y T P U X Q L P Q R N M K W
N F Z G C P U E I S T E R W D A C O R O A N V R Y
G F C P F Y R H S H I W B H M S K S A P K U Y V W
W X W E K U E Z H V C E H U K C G N B S S M E K H
Q G L O B A L I Z A T I O N Y I M F V L G U T W I
Z I K F I A B R K A X E O L N H R M B F Z N P Y K
Q S J R M V C I W D V P T R A N S N A T I O N A L
```

Comparative   Cyberterrorism   Domestic   Ethnocentrism   FTO   Globalization

Infrastructure   Smuggling   International   Trafficking   Transnational

Crossword Puzzle

Across

3. Premeditated politically motivated violence perpetrated against noncombatant targets by subnational groups or clandestine agents.

8. The phenomenon of "culture-centeredness".

9. _____ criminology focuses on the cross-national study of crime.

10. Sex _____ involves the recruitment, harboring, transportation, provision, or obtaining of a person for the purpose of a commercial sex act.

Down

1. A process of social homogenization.

2. The basic facilities, services, and installations needed for a community to function.

4. _____ uses high technology to plan and carry out terrorist attacks.

5. _____ involves illegal immigration using a paid agent to help someone clandestinely cross a border.

6. _____ terrorism is committed by a group or individual with a connection to a foreign power or whose activities transcend national boundaries.

7. _____ terrorism is committed by groups or individuals based and operating entirely within the United States.

Epilogue

Learning Outcomes

After reading this Epilogue, students should be able to:

- Describe futures research and explain some of the techniques used for assessing the future
- Identify some possible future crimes and explain how criminal activity in the future may differ from criminal activity today
- List and describe some specific predictions about the future of criminological theorizing
- Outline some possible crime-control policies of the future and explain why new strategies may be necessary
- Provide an informed opinion as to whether the crime problem can ultimately be solved

Chapter Outline

Introduction
Techniques of Futures Research
Future Crimes
The New Criminologies
Policies of the Future
Can We Solve the Problem of Crime?
    Symbolism and Public Policy

Chapter Summary

People who study the future are known as futurists. Future criminology is the study of likely futures as they relate to crime and its control. There are many groups who study the future; organizations such as the Society of Police Futurists International specifically focus on future crime-control policy.

Futures research is a multidisciplinary branch of operations research that attempts to facilitate long-range planning based on four elements: forecasting from the past supported by mathematical models; cross-disciplinary treatment of its subject matter; systematic use of expert judgment; and a systems-analytical approach to its problems. Futures research, which requires a futurist perspective, uses seven main techniques: trend extrapolation, cross-impact analysis, the Delphi Method, simulations and models, environmental scanning, scenario writing, and strategic assessment. They all provide an appreciation of the risks and opportunities facing those planning for the future. Regardless of the technique, the results are no better than the data used.

Most futurists suggest that although traditional crimes (murder, rape, robbery, etc.) will continue to occur in the future, other new and emergent forms of criminality will increase in number and frequency. New types of criminality predicted by futurists include computer-based and economic crime, identity manipulation, and the increasing involvement of organized crime in toxic and nuclear waste disposal. Georgette Bennett, who helped establish the study of criminal futures as a purposeful endeavor, has predicted a number of areas of coming change, including a decline in street crime and an increase in white-collar and high-technology crimes; increasing involvement of females and the elderly in crime; and safer cities, with an increase in criminal activity in small towns and rural areas.

In addition to futures research, new and emerging criminological theories help suggest what criminology will be like in the future. During the 1980s and 1990s, a number of new and dynamic theories were developed, such as postmodernism, feminist criminology, and peacemaking criminology. One new perspective is David Farrington's risk factor prevention paradigm. This paradigm, which emphasizes identifying the key risk factors for offending and implementing prevention methods designed to counteract them, became increasingly influential in criminology during the 1990s.

For policymakers to be able to plan for the future, they need as much information as possible about possible eventualities. The increasingly multicultural and heterogeneous nature of the United States will also affect crime, as it will increase anomie. Diverse heterogeneous societies, such as the United States, experience constant internal conflict. Disagreement about the law and social norms is common, and offenders tend to deny responsibility and to attempt to avoid capture and conviction. Richter Moore, Jr., has identified seven issues that he suggests are likely to concern crime-control planners in the near future.

Currently, many criminologists expect to work closely with politicians and policymakers to develop crime-control agendas based on scientific knowledge and criminological theorizing. Many critics feel that the only way to address the issues underlying high crime rates is to implement drastic policy-level changes, such as drug legalization, the elimination of guns throughout the country, nightly curfews, and close control of media violence. These reforms may be unlikely because of cultural taboos rooted in citizens' demands for individual freedoms. Because of this, many feel that there may not be a solution to the crime problem. Some even suggest that crime-control policies are largely symbolic and that crime will always be a part of our society.

Key Concepts

Cross-impact analysis: A technique of futures research that attempts to analyze one trend or event in light of the occurrence or nonoccurrence of a series of related events.

Delphi Method: A technique of futures research that uses repetitive questioning of experts to refine predictions.

Environmental scanning: "A systematic effort to identify in an elemental way future developments (trends or events) that could plausibly occur over the time horizon of interest" and that might affect one's area of concern.

Future criminology: The study of likely futures as they impinge on crime and its control.

Futures research: "A multidisciplinary branch of operations research" whose principal aim "is to facilitate long-range planning based on (1) forecasting from the past supported by mathematical models, (2) cross-disciplinary treatment of its subject matter, (3) systematic use of expert judgment, and (4) a systems-analytical approach to its problems."

Futurist: One who studies the future.

Kriminalpolitik: The political handling of crime. Also, a criminology-based social policy.

Scenario writing: A technique, intended to predict future outcomes, that builds upon environmental scanning by attempting to assess the likelihood of a variety of possible outcomes once important trends have been identified.

Strategic assessment: A technique that assesses the risks and opportunities facing those who plan for the future.

Trend extrapolation: A technique of futures research that makes future predictions based on the projection of existing trends.

Questions for Review

1. What is futures research? Explain some of the techniques used by futurists for assessing the future.
2. List and describe some possible future crimes and tell how they might differ from the kinds of criminal activity that we are familiar with today.
3. What are some of the specific predictions about the future of criminological theorizing that this chapter offers?
4. Why might new crime-fighting strategies be necessary in the future? What kinds of innovative crime-control strategies might the future bring?
5. Can the problem of crime be solved? If so, how? If not, why not?

Questions for Reflection

1. This book emphasizes a social problems versus social responsibility theme. Which perspective do you think will be dominant in twenty-first-century crime-control planning? Why?
2. Do you believe that it is possible to know the future? What techniques are identified in this chapter for assessing possible futures? Which of these do you think holds the most promise? Why?
3. What kinds of crime-control policies do you think the future will bring? Will they be consistent with present understandings of civil liberties? Why or why not?

Student Exercises

Activity #1

Your instructor will place you into groups. The text outlines several crime-related issues that may be key issues for policymakers over the next ten years. Each group will identify three additional issues they believe may be of concern in the future. Groups may compare and contrast the items on their lists. Focus on the wide range of issues that are present among a fairly homogeneous group of people.

Activity #2

Write a short paper in which you identify the crime-related issues that are today's "hot buttons" or issues of major social and political concern. Which of these do you think will still be hot topics ten years in the future? Explain why you think these issues will remain at the forefront of American consciousness and continue to create challenges for criminal justice.

Criminology Today on the Web

www.wfs.org

This is the home page of the World Future Society.

www.policefuturists.org

This is the home page of the Society of Police Futurists International.

www.foresight.gov.uk

This is the home page of the U.K.'s government-led Foresight program.

www.fbi.gov/hq/td/fwg/workhome.htm

This is the home page of the FBI's Futures Working Group.

www.futures.hawaii.edu

This is the home page of the Hawaii Research Center for Futures Studies.

www.forecastingprinciples.com/

This Web site presents a summary of useful knowledge about forecasting.

www.altfutures.com

This is the home page of the Institute for Alternative Futures.

Student Study Guide Questions

True/False

_____ 1. Futurists primarily focus on how crime will appear in the distant future.

_____ 2. From the present point of view, multiple futures exist.

_____ 3. The journal, *The Futurist*, is published by the World Future Society.

_____ 4. Members of the Society of Police Futurists International apply the principles of futures research to understand the world as it is likely to be in the future.

_____ 5. According to Foresight's Crime Prevention Panel, traditional family forms will decline over the next few decades.

_____ 6. According to Foresight's Crime Prevention Panel, local crimes will be replaced by crimes with a global scope.

_____ 7. According to the futurist perspective, distinct trends and developments cannot be ignored.

_____ 8. Demographic and economic models are sometimes used to predict future criminality.

_____ 9. Environmental scanning provides an appreciation of the risks and opportunities facing those who plan for the future.

_____ 10. Scenario writers focus on predicting a specific future.

_____ 11. Futurist Richter Moore, Jr. suggests that identity theft will be a nexus of future crime.

_____ 12. Futurist Georgette Bennett predicts an increase in street crime.

_____ 13. Some criminological theories have been significantly more effective than others in explaining, predicting, and controlling crime.

_____ 14. According to futurist L. Edward Wells, future explanations of crime will more greatly emphasize biological factors.

_____ 15. In a heterogeneous society, citizens tend to share backgrounds, life experiences, and values.

_____ 16. Heterogeneous societies suffer from constant internal conflict.

_____ 17. The United States is an advanced heterogeneous society.

_____ 18. Richter Moore, Jr. suggests that in the future, there will be a greater emphasis on the treatment of criminality.

Fill in the Blank

19. The book _Megatrends_ was written by futurist _____.

20. According to Foresight's Crime Prevention Panel, Web sites written in _____ will be the most likely to be targeted.

21. According to Foresight's Crime Prevention Panel, technology is leading to the growth of a(n) _____ society.

22. Globalization refers to the increasingly _____ characterization of social life.

23. According to the _____ perspective, there are alternative futures.

24. _____ makes future predictions based on the projection of existing trends.

25. The first step of the Delphi Method is _____.

26. _____ is a technique of futures research that builds upon environmental scanning.

27. Crimes that have the widest negative effects are known as _____ crimes.

28. Georgette Bennett has predicted that high crime rates will shift from the _____ Belt to the _____ Belt.

29. L. Edward Wells predicts that future explanations of crime will be predominantly _____ rather than collective.

30. David Farrington developed the _____ paradigm.

31. Gene Stephens suggests that crime will _____ worldwide in the future.

32. According to Gene Stephens, multiculturalism and heterogeneity increase _____.

33. In some _____ societies, offenders who break norms will often punish themselves, even if their transgressions are not publicly discovered.

34. _____ was the first country to experience the crime problems associated with anomie.

35. The concept of _____ refers to a criminology-based social policy.

36. Some analysts suggest that federal crime-control policies are largely _____, rather than actual attempts to reduce crime.

Multiple Choice

37. Assumptions about the future may be based on
    a. existing and highly credible public or private statistics.
    b. mathematical analyses of trends.
    c. the integration of diverse materials from many different sources.
    d. All of the above

38. John Naisbitt wrote
    a. *Future Shock.*
    b. *Crimewarps.*
    c. *Megatrends.*
    d. *Our Posthuman Future.*

39. Well-known futurist _____ is the author of *Future Shock.*
    a. Alvin Toffler
    b. John Naisbitt
    c. Peter Drucker
    d. William Tafoya

40. The Futures Working Group is a joint venture by the FBI and the
    a. World Future Society.
    b. Society of Police Futurists International
    c. Foresight Program
    d. None of the above

41. The _____ is run by the government of the United Kingdom.
    a. Society of Police Futurists International
    b. World Future Society
    c. Foresight Program
    d. None of the above

42. Futures research facilitates long-range planning based on all but which of the following?
    a. Cross-disciplinary treatment of its subject matter
    b. Systematic use of expert judgment
    c. Forecasting from the past supported by mathematical models
    d. Evaluations based on public opinion

43. Which of the following is not one of the main techniques of futures research?
    a. The Delphi Method
    b. Scenario writing
    c. Cross-cultural surveys
    d. Trend extrapolation

44. The technique of futures research that attempts to analyze one trend or event in light of the occurrence or nonoccurrence of a series of related events is known as
    a. trend extrapolation.
    b. the Delphi Method.
    c. scenario writing.
    d. cross-impact analysis.

45. The technique of futures research that involves a targeted effort to collect as much information as possible in a systematic effort to identify in an elemental way future developments that could plausibly occur over the time horizon of interest is
    a. the Delphi Method.
    b. trend extrapolation.
    c. environmental scanning.
    d. scenario writing.

46. The technique of futures research that provides an appreciation of the risks and opportunities facing those who plan for the future is
    a. strategic assessment.
    b. trend extrapolation.
    c. cross-impact analysis.
    d. simulations and models.

47. The book *Crimewarps* was written by futurist
    a. Richter Moore, Jr.
    b. Georgette Bennett.
    c. Peter Drucker.
    d. William Tafoya.

48. According to predictions made by Georgette Bennett, cities will
    a. become safer.
    b. become more dangerous.
    c. have relatively stable crime rates.
    d. Bennett did not make any predictions about cities.

49. According to L. Edward Wells, theoretical changes may be brought about by
    a. legal events.
    b. significant social change.
    c. advances in scientific knowledge.
    d. All of the above

50. According to futurist L. Edward Wells, future explanations of crime will be more
    a. eclectic.
    b. comparative.
    c. applied.
    d. All of the above

51. A new era of theory building in criminology began in the
    a. 1960s.
    b. 1970s.
    c. 1980s.
    d. 1990s.

52. According to David P. Farrington, which of the following is not one of the main challenges for the risk factor prevention paradigm?
    a. Determining what risk factors are causes
    b. Establishing what are the protective factors
    c. Assessing the monetary costs and benefits of interventions
    d. Developing new theoretical constructs

53. Which of the following is not typically the norm in a homogeneous society?
    a. A tradition of discipline
    b. A belief in the laws
    c. An acceptance of personal responsibility
    d. Cultural diversity

54. According to Gene Stephens, _____ in societies will be the rule in the twenty-first century.
    a. homogeneity
    b. heterogeneity
    c. cultural monotheism
    d. reduced diversity

Word Search Puzzle

```
O S L G N H Y K R H X M T R S J M T R E N D A A J
W S X W L M K U Q U G I U V O Z B K R S Y Y H Y N
Y B Y P G R D C F W R X P S C B R R F D P D R S V
L U B H K W J I F W C P K Q R A R I S X H O W N H
C D Q K R O L J Y W W B Q G O N A M V H I Z C V X
K E D L N E I N A C L P X H S T B I H P Z C J H F
M L S F U N L F X C R G G E S M B N T G G M T X F
A P W I X V B V U V P Q Z P I K Y A H E Q S D M Q
P H M U T I Z E N R K O T X M C M L A B T W N U Z
U I F A P R K G H E W P O M P W R P Z M D B K J C
A N Y T L O N S U B E Q J E A B D O E G T U Q K X
T O M L K N Z T N S W Z U J C P Y L E T M O S D P
T R R E I M H K T L V G S J T M F I D J T T F M Y
S G R J S E G P K T I K I N A K Z T V X J C R P Z
H V H D T N K M N V Q I D U X I I N T Y U H C C I
F T Z U H T Q Z V P V C T J T B T K S C F Y M N I
B R O K O A Q I H G M Q G O C E Z O C H U H M C D
H T A Z C L D L G Z K D J P J C R A E Y T M G T V
X Z Y C C A J N I V X H U B K T D O N M U X V O B
M A P C P N Y C D J E Q H Y H N W S A H R P W Y R
C B X C H T C T T U N I Q A W E B P R P I B K P O
W H U V D X U X E S O O H C G Q V M I F S I U L K
L G R E M N W B I Z Y D I M T H U F O A T E W O E
F P Z J P W S T R A T E G I C U F P G D K V J O N
F C V L J A T Y I L Y E A D X H J D P X S M A X D
```

| Cross-impact | Delphi | Environmental | Futurist | Kriminalpolitik | Scenario |
| Strategic | Trend | | | | |

Crossword Puzzle

Across

3. _____ writing attempts to assess the likelihood of a variety of possible outcomes once important trends have been identified.

4. _____ analysis attempts to analyze one trend or event in light of the occurrence or nonoccurrence of a series of related events.

6. The _____ Method uses repetitive questioning of experts to refine predictions.

7. _____ criminology is the study of likely futures as they impinge on crime and its control.

8. _____ assessment assesses the risks and opportunities facing those who plan for the future.

Down

1. Trend _____ makes future predictions based on the projection of existing trends.

2. _____ scanning identifies future developments that could occur over a time period of interest.

5. One who studies the future.

Answers to Student Study Guide Questions

Chapter 1

1. True
2. False
3. False
4. True
5. False
6. False
7. False
8. False
9. False
10. False
11. True
12. False
13. False
14. False
15. False
16. False
17. False
18. False
19. legalistic
20. illegal
21. antisocial
22. maladaptive
23. Deviant behavior
24. consensus
25. criminalist
26. spirit possession
27. Paul Topinard
28. Criminology
29. profession
30. criminal justice
31. unicausal
32. macro
33. individual
34. outputs
35. foreground
36. social phenomenon
37. b
38. a
39. c
40. c
41. d
42. b
43. d
44. c
45. a
46. a
47. b
48. a
49. a
50. b
51. a
52. a
53. b
54. c

Chapter 2

1. False
2. False
3. False
4. True
5. False
6. False
7. False
8. True
9. False
10. False
11. True
12. False
13. True
14. False
15. True
16. True
17. False
18. False
19. Thomas Robert Malthus
20. decrease
21. cleared
22. dark figure of crime
23. FBI
24. one-half
25. Homicide
26. Criminal homicide
27. power
28. strong-arm
29. decreasing steadily
30. Crime Awareness and Campus Security Act
31. increases
32. Women
33. socially significant
34. correlation
35. six
36. correlation
37. c
38. b
39. b
40. c
41. c
42. b
43. a
44. d
45. a
46. b
47. a
48. c
49. c
50. c
51. a
52. b
53. b
54. b

Chapter 3

1. False
2. True
3. True
4. True
5. False
6. False
7. False
8. True
9. False

10. True
11. False
12. False
13. True
14. True
15. False
16. False
17. True
18. False
19. theory
20. patterns
21. frameworks
22. applied
23. hypothesis
24. confounding effects
25. external
26. History
27. Experimental mortality
28. self-selection
29. internal
30. life history
31. Secondary analysis
32. validity
33. analysis
34. median
35. decreases
36. title page
37. a
38. a
39. c
40. c
41. b
42. c
43. a
44. a
45. d
46. c
47. b
48. a
49. b
50. d
51. d
52. c
53. d
54. d

Chapter 4

1. True
2. False
3. False
4. False
5. True

6. False
7. False
8. True
9. False
10. False
11. True
12. True
13. True
14. False
15. True
16. True
17. True
18. False
19. laws
20. *in se*
21. Code of Hammurabi
22. Edward the Confessor
23. natural law
24. useless
25. punishment
26. Hard
27. justice
28. rational choice
29. reducing rewards
30. opportunity
31. event
32. just deserts
33. Recidivism
34. Truth in sentencing
35. incapacitation
36. Collective incapacitation
37. d
38. b
39. d
40. d
41. d
42. b
43. b
44. c
45. c
46. c
47. c
48. b
49. b
50. a
51. d
52. b
53. b
54. d

Chapter 5

1. True
2. False
3. True
4. True
5. False
6. False
7. False
8. False
9. False
10. True
11. True
12. True
13. False
14. False
15. True
16. True
17. False
18. True
19. constitutionally/genetically
20. gender
21. skull
22. Earnest Hooton
23. Constitutional/somatotype
24. hypoglycemia
25. enhancing
26. pink
27. serotonin
28. positive
29. Juke
30. Eugenic
31. *Buck* v. *Bell*
32. Sir Francis Galton
33. monozygotic
34. territoriality
35. low
36. C. Ray Jeffery
37. b
38. b
39. d
40. b
41. a
42. a
43. b
44. b
45. d
46. a
47. d
48. b
49. a
50. a
51. c

52. a
53. d
54. c

Chapter 6

1. True
2. False
3. False
4. True
5. False
6. True
7. True
8. True
9. False
10. True
11. False
12. True
13. True
14. False
15. False
16. False
17. False
18. False
19. Forensic
20. sociopath
21. Somatogenic
22. psychogenic
23. two-thirds
24. Psychiatric
25. id
26. ego
27. functional
28. imitation
29. Behavior
30. attachment
31. Self-control
32. low
33. John Hinkley
34. defendant
35. disease
36. substantial capacity test
37. c
38. c
39. d
40. b
41. b
42. d
43. a
44. b
45. d
46. d
47. d
48. c
49. c
50. b
51. c
52. b
53. c
54. d

Chapter 7

1. False
2. False
3. False
4. True
5. True
6. True
7. False
8. False
9. False
10. True
11. True
12. True
13. False
14. True
15. False
16. True
17. False
18. True
19. process
20. disorganization/pathology
21. V
22. environmental
23. Defensible space
24. anomie
25. conformity
26. ritualism
27. relative deprivation
28. primary
29. Walter Miller
30. denying injury
31. subculture of violence
32. adolescent through middle age
33. legitimate
34. deviance
35. respect
36. responsibility
37. a
38. d
39. a
40. b
41. b
42. d
43. d
44. a
45. a
46. a
47. b
48. a
49. b
50. d
51. c
52. a
53. a
54. a

Chapter 8

1. False
2. False
3. False
4. False
5. False
6. True
7. False
8. True
9. True
10. False
11. True
12. True
13. False
14. False
15. False
16. True
17. True
18. True
19. reinforcement
20. inner
21. psychopath
22. control ratio
23. tagging
24. Primary
25. pure
26. Stigmatic
27. Reintegrative
28. Duration
29. trajectory
30. acceleration
31. human agency
32. social capital
33. life course persisters
34. adolescence-limited
35. ecological
36. 11 or 12
37. b
38. c
39. b

40. b
41. b
42. c
43. b
44. a
45. c
46. c
47. d
48. c
49. d
50. a
51. a
52. b
53. b
54. d

Chapter 9

1. False
2. True
3. True
4. False
5. False
6. True
7. True
8. False
9. True
10. True
11. False
12. True
13. False
14. False
15. True
16. True
17. False
18. False
19. consensus
20. pluralistic
21. bourgeoisie
22. achieved
23. political
24. absence
25. Instrumental
26. Radical
27. Walter DeKeseredy
28. left realism
29. Patriarchy
30. Rita Simon
31. power-control
32. deconstructionist
33. constitutive
34. peace
35. peacemaking

36. dispute resolution
37. a
38. c
39. a
40. c
41. a
42. c
43. a
44. d
45. c
46. b
47. c
48. a
49. b
50. c
51. d
52. a
53. c
54. a

Chapter 10

1. False
2. False
3. True
4. False
5. False
6. False
7. False
8. True
9. True
10. False
11. False
12. False
13. True
14. True
15. True
16. True
17. True
18. False
19. single-variable
20. Primary
21. precipitation
22. three
23. financial gain/material gain
24. visionary
25. organized nonsocial
26. facilitator
27. Rape shield
28. male
29. power
30. social disorganization
31. power-reassurance

32. peer
33. deniers
34. robbery
35. Assault
36. Cyberstalking
37. c
38. c
39. a
40. c
41. d
42. c
43. a
44. d
45. d
46. d
47. c
48. c
49. b
50. a
51. d
52. c
53. b
54. d

Chapter 11

1. False
2. True
3. True
4. False
5. True
6. False
7. True
8. False
9. False
10. False
11. False
12. True
13. True
14. True
15. False
16. False
17. False
18. True
19. persistent
20. break-in
21. Larceny
22. stripping
23. teenagers
24. boredom
25. impulsive
26. semiprofessional
27. enigma

28. 72
29. high-level
30. suitability
31. four
32. robbery
33. Fetish
34. specialist
35. noncovered
36. 1996
37. c
38. b
39. a
40. b
41. a
42. b
43. a
44. b
45. a
46. c
47. b
48. c
49. a
50. c
51. b
52. b
53. c
54. a

Chapter 12

1. False
2. True
3. True
4. False
5. False
6. False
7. False
8. True
9. True
10. True
11. True
12. True
13. True
14. False
15. False
16. True
17. False
18. True
19. high
20. violator
21. professional
22. accountability
23. Clayton

24. political
25. Camorra
26. Ethnic
27. consolidate
28. *U.S.* v. *Bufalino*
29. 24
30. underboss
31. lieutenants/caporegime
32. five
33. Outfit
34. Latino
35. Hobbs
36. Money laundering
37. b
38. a
39. c
40. b
41. b
42. d
43. b
44. c
45. a
46. d
47. c
48. a
49. a
50. c
51. b
52. a
53. b
54. d

Chapter 13

1. False
2. True
3. True
4. True
5. True
6. False
7. True
8. True
9. False
10. True
11. True
12. False
13. False
14. True
15. True
16. True
17. False
18. True
19. Psychoactive

20. drug induced
21. Stimulants
22. marijuana
23. hallucinogen
24. doctor shopping
25. pipelines
26. 1907
27. 1906
28. Harrison
29. Volsted
30. Marijuana Tax
31. heroin
32. Legalization
33. call girl
34. john
35. sex work
36. Decriminalization
37. c
38. c
39. c
40. d
41. d
42. a
43. c
44. c
45. a
46. b
47. d
48. c
49. b
50. c
51. a
52. a
53. d
54. b

Chapter 14

1. True
2. False
3. False
4. False
5. False
6. False
7. False
8. False
9. False
10. False
11. False
12. True
13. False
14. False
15. False

16. False
17. False
18. True
19. trespass
20. Defense
21. Warez
22. Softlifting
23. virus
24. property
25. First
26. cyberspace
27. scamps
28. Game players
29. identity theft
30. Existing
31. CAD/computer-aided dispatch
32. British
33. AFIS/automated fingerprint identification system
34. expert
35. Threat analysis
36. Computer Fraud and Abuse
37. c
38. c
39. b
40. d
41. a
42. b
43. c
44. a
45. c
46. a
47. d
48. b
49. d
50. a
51. c
52. b
53. d
54. a

Chapter 15

1. True
2. True
3. False
4. True
5. False
6. True
7. False
8. False
9. True
10. False

11. False
12. True
13. True
14. False
15. True
16. False
17. False
18. False
19. Transnational
20. Trafficking in persons/TIP
21. 18
22. Comparative
23. Ethnocentrism
24. China
25. civilians
26. Anarchist
27. International
28. domestic
29. Cyberterrorism
30. GovNet
31. Biological terrorism/bioterrorism
32. Tom Ridge
33. five
34. Emergency Preparedness and Response/EPR
35. U.S. Department of State
36. WMDs
37. b
38. d
39. d
40. c
41. c
42. d
43. a
44. c
45. c
46. a
47. d
48. b
49. c
50. a
51. d
52. a
53. b
54. d

Epilogue

1. False
2. True
3. True
4. True

5. True
6. True
7. True
8. True
9. False
10. False
11. True
12. False
13. False
14. True
15. False
16. True
17. True
18. True
19. John Naisbitt
20. English
21. impersonal
22. international
23. futurist
24. Trend extrapolation
25. problem identification
26. Scenario writing
27. socially significant
28. Frost; Sun
29. individualistic
30. risk factor prevention
31. increase
32. anomie
33. homogenous
34. The United States
35. *Kriminalpolitik*
36. symbolic
37. d
38. c
39. a
40. b
41. c
42. c
43. c
44. d
45. c
46. a
47. b
48. a
49. d
50. d
51. c
52. d
53. d
54. b